# Etowah River User's Guide

# Etowah River User's Guide
## Joe Cook

GEORGIA RIVER NETWORK GUIDEBOOKS

Published in Cooperation with the Coosa River Basin Initiative

The University of Georgia Press    Athens & London

GEORGIA
RIVER
NETWORK
GUIDEBOOKS

© 2013 by the University of Georgia Press

Athens, Georgia 30602

www.ugapress.org

All rights reserved

Designed by Omega Clay

Set in Quadraat serif and sans by Omega Clay

Manufactured by Everbest for Four Colour Print Group

Printed in China

17 16 15 14 13  P  5 4 3 2 1

Library of Congress Cataloging-in-Publication Data

Cook, Joe, 1966–

Etowah river user's guide / Joe Cook.

p. cm. — (Georgia River Network guidebooks)

"Published in cooperation with the Coosa River Basin Initiative."

ISBN 978-0-8203-4463-8 (pbk. : alk. paper) —

ISBN 0-8203-4463-X (pbk. : alk. paper)

1. Boats and boating—Georgia—Etowah River—Guidebooks.

2. Outdoor recreation—Georgia—Etowah River—Guidebooks.

3. Etowah River (Ga.)—Guidebooks.  I. Title.

GV776.G42E762 2013

797.109758—dc23      2012030433

British Library Cataloging-in-Publication Data available

# Contents

## THE RIVER

# Contents

# Acknowledgments

Compiling the information contained in this book would not have been possible without the many individuals and entities that provided advice and support. I thank Chris Worick and Anne Amerson for their insight into the history of Lumpkin County, David Archer of Cartersville for providing a wealth of information about the Etowah in Bartow County, Russell McClanahan of the Rome History Museum for feeding me facts about Rome's rivers, and Jeff Bishop of the Georgia Trail of Tears Association for assisting with facts about the Etowah's Native inhabitants. The Georgia Canoeing Association and its members, especially Roger Nott, provided critical information about the upper Etowah. My paddling companions Joe "Doc" Stephens, Vincent Payne, and April Ingle accompanied me on several cold-weather scouting trips, and Elliot Johnson of Lilydipper Outfitters in Canton helped map the river's headwaters during a rainy hike from the spring that begins the river. Thanks also to Diane Minick of the Upper Etowah River Alliance and Matthew Pate of Forsyth County Parks and Recreation Department for their tireless work in creating the Etowah River Water Trail and reviewing the contents of this book, Paul Diprima of the Coosa Valley Chapter of Trout Unlimited for contributing the fishing primer, and Mary and Bud Freeman of the University of Georgia and Henning Von Schmeling of the Chattahoochee Nature Center for their advice in compiling the book's natural history section.

The creation of the maps for this book, as well as the Etowah River Water Trail website (www.etowahwatertrail.org), was made possible through a generous grant from the Lyndhurst Foundation.

We thank the UGA Press staff, especially Regan Huff, for shepherding this project, and the board, staff, members, and volunteers of the Coosa River Basin Initiative and the Georgia River Network for providing the support to make compiling this book possible. And, finally, thanks to GRN board member Dorinda Dallmeyer, who first envisioned a series of guidebooks to Georgia's rivers.

## Map Legend

★ **Point of Interest**

◎ **Shoal/Rapid**

▣ **Fish Weir**

⊗ **Water Intake/Discharge**

. **River Mile Marker**

■ **River Gauge**

▲ **Campground**

⚓ **Marina**

⊙ **Outfitter**

⛆ **Take Out/Launch Site**

▨ **Federal Land**

▨ **State Land**

The map above provides an overview of
the length of the river, detailing sections
covered on individual maps included
in this book. The symbols included in
the legend are used on individual maps
throughout the guide.

# Etowah River User's Guide

# Introduction

As Georgia rivers go, the Etowah is a bit contrary. While the Savannah and Chattahoochee, which share the Etowah's Appalachian Mountain birthing suite, are content to roll southeast and southwest following the gentle slope of the state's geology through the Piedmont and on to the Coastal Plain, the Etowah takes an unusual path. Like its neighbors to the east, it starts south, but when it reaches the Piedmont, it takes an odd turn to the northwest and goes on a meandering journey through Northwest Georgia's Ridge and Valley region. No other river lying entirely within Georgia's boundaries flows on such a northwest course.

It begins its life about 2,800 feet above sea level as a tiny spring on the southern slope of the Tennessee Valley Divide some 15 miles northwest of Dahlonega. From there it splashes down off the divide, descending 1,400 feet in its first 7 miles. Its pace then slows, spreading some 800 feet of descent over the next 150 miles.

Along the way it flows through six counties and drains portions of five others. Viewed from space it gives the appearance of a confused and frightened snake, coiling and slithering here and there as if it can't decide which way to go. The communities through which it passes might well be characterized the same way. On the fringes of Atlanta's burgeoning suburbs, the residents of Dahlonega, Dawsonville, Canton, Cartersville, Rome, and other smaller hamlets live in a rapidly changing river basin where rural countryside is steadily being overtaken by a suburban landscape.

From 1991 to 2005, portions of the Etowah's drainage basin closest to Atlanta lost an average of 50 acres of forests and fields each day, and the vast majority of that greenspace was replaced with asphalt, concrete, and buildings—an alarming trend for the Etowah and its tributaries. Scientists have shown that the richness and diversity of stream communities in the Etowah has declined with the ever-urbanizing landscape.

And, in the Etowah, there is much to lose. Though small in size (draining only 1,860 square miles), the Etowah is among the most biologically rich rivers in the country. It is estimated that the Etowah basin, with its 75 native species of fish, has more imperiled species (17 fish species and 16 invertebrate species) than any other river system of its size in the southeastern United States. By comparison, the Colorado River, with a 246,000-square-mile watershed, hosts only 25 native fish species; the Columbia, with a 258,000-square-mile watershed, hosts 33 native fish species. Indeed, the Etowah is a key link in Southeast's claim as the cradle of North American aquatic biodiversity.

Of particular concern are the federally endangered amber and Etowah darters and the federally threatened Cherokee darter. Cherokee and Etowah darters are found nowhere else in the world. These brightly colored, 2- to 3-inch members of the perch family make their home in shoal habitats found in the Etowah and its tributaries.

While siltation and stormwater in the rapidly growing region threaten to spoil their habitat, perhaps the biggest threat to these and other fish of the Etowah is dams and manmade reservoirs. Lovers of free-flowing streams, the darters cannot survive in lake habitats. The dams also alter habitat downstream and permanently isolate fish communities. The only impoundment on the mainstem of the Etowah, the U.S. Army Corps of Engineers' Lake Allatoona, dramatically illustrates the impacts wrought by dams.

The Etowah downstream from Allatoona suffers from low oxygen levels, altered temperatures, and extreme fluctuations in flows. Since the dam was completed in 1950, mussel and fish populations in the river have steadily declined. Historically, 80 fish species appeared in the Etowah below Allatoona; today only 45 remain. The impacts have been even more devastating for the river's mussel fauna. Prior to construction of Allatoona, as many as 27 species could be found in the river; today, none survive.

Currently, there are more than 3,000 smaller impoundments in the Etowah River basin, ranging from small farm ponds to large amenity lakes—each having similar impacts on a smaller scale. And more reservoirs are being planned; in 2012, nine new water supply reservoirs were in the planning stages.

ETOWAH NEAR REYNOLDS BEND, FLOYD COUNTY

Compounding the impacts of these water supply projects is the fact that many of them involve "interbasin transfers" in which water is pumped from the Etowah or its tributaries and piped to homes and businesses in Metro Atlanta, where it is used and released to the Chattahoochee River, robbing the Etowah and downstream communities of that flow. Not surprisingly, interbasin transfers have become one of the most controversial water supply options in Georgia, and the Etowah, owing to its proximity to Metro Atlanta, sits at the epicenter of the interbasin transfer debate.

For all this swirling modern-day controversy, the Etowah remains a portal to the past. The richness of the Native American history along its shores (and within the river channel itself) is unsurpassed in Georgia. The Etowah Indian Mounds State Historic Site in Cartersville, home to several thousand Native Americans from AD 1000 to AD 1550, is considered the most intact Mississippian Culture site in the Southeast. The three mounds that rise above the river there overlook a fish weir constructed by these inhabitants to corral and catch fish. That weir is one of more than 40 such structures bisecting the Etowah. In fact, more weirs can be found on the Etowah than on all other Georgia rivers combined.

These Native Americans gave way to white settlers in the early 19th century. When gold was discovered along the Etowah in 1828, sparking the nation's first gold rush, the fate of the Native cultures in Georgia was sealed. By the late 1830s, soldiers at "removal forts" located along the Etowah were rounding up the Native peoples and forcibly removing them west.

FISH WEIR NEAR GA. 113, BARTOW COUNTY

The gold rush, though relatively short lived, left an indelible mark on the river. As mining techniques advanced, entire hillsides were blasted away using "giants," high-pressured hydraulic water hoses. The resulting mud and silt coursed to the Etowah and its feeder streams, along with the mercury used in the process of extracting the gold.

During the Civil War, the Etowah was so strategic in Union general William T. Sherman's march to Atlanta that he dubbed it "the Rubicon of Georgia." The sole railroad bridge over the Etowah near Cartersville was burned by retreating Confederate troops and rebuilt by Union soldiers in just six days. The town of Etowah, located where Allatoona Dam sits today, saw its ironworks destroyed. Likewise, on the banks of the Etowah in Rome, the Noble Foundry, maker of Confederate canons, was burned.

However, its importance during the Civil War is surpassed by its impact on the hamlets that crowd its banks. The Etowah is inextricably linked to the culture and progress of those who have suffered through its droughts and battled its floods. From the first grist and gold stamp mills of Dawson County in the 19th century to Cartersville's first source of electricity, the circa 1900 Thompson Weinman Dam, the Etowah has blessed these communities.

LAKE ALLATOONA, BARTOW COUNTY

Even its floods, which especially ravaged Rome periodically until the construction of Allatoona Dam, perversely prompted "progress." One of North Georgia's most celebrated moonshiners of the 20th century is said to have gotten his start in the business after a freshet made his bottomland corn crop unusable except in the production of illicit whiskey.

Today, the river remains a work horse. It supplies 10 percent of Metro Atlanta's drinking water and is the primary source of water for about one million people in Dawson, Cherokee, Bartow, Cobb, Paulding, and Floyd Counties. It fills Lake Allatoona, where the recreation and tourism industry pumps an estimated $93 million into the local economy annually. The dam that creates that lake supplies enough electricity to light 17,000 homes each year, and just downstream its water fuels Georgia Power Company's Plant Bowen, one of the nation's largest coal-fired power plants. The river doesn't stop there. Even the sand that has been used to condition the Atlanta Braves playing diamond at Turner Field comes from the Etowah and the Blankenship Sand Company.

This river, it's a giver. And, that is why we come to it. For all it doles out to us, perhaps its greatest gift is the opportunity to lose ourselves on its watery path—to experience its wildness, beauty, and peacefulness. This book is an invitation to this place. Our hope is that in exploring and understanding the Etowah, you, the reader, will return the gift by caring for and keeping this river for future generations.

# Safety

A year does not pass in which someone does not drown on the Etowah River or Lake Allatoona. Despite its billing as "the best family paddling" in North Georgia, the Etowah, like all rivers, is not without its dangers. Rivers are unforgiving of our carelessness. Being properly prepared for your excursion and abiding by safe boating practices (including state boating laws) will reduce your risk of mistakes and keep you coming back to the river time after time.

## Wear Your Life Jacket

This is the No. 1 rule of boating safety. PFDs—personal flotation devices—are known as "life jackets" for a reason: they save lives. Wear a PFD or run the risk of being DOA. Georgia state law requires that all vessels have at least one U.S. Coast

ROCK ISLAND, REYNOLDS BEND, FLOYD COUNTY

Guard–approved Type I, II, III, or V PFD for each person on board. However, Type V PFDs are acceptable only when worn and securely fastened. Children under the age of 10 must wear a life jacket at all times on a moving vessel.

Though state law doesn't require it, wearing your life jacket at all times is the best practice.

## Know Your Boat

Whether you are in a canoe, kayak, paddleboard, or motorized boat, know how to operate your vessel. Canoe and kayaking classes are taught by numerous organizations. The Georgia Canoeing Association, http://www.gapaddle.com/, teaches regular classes on paddling and boating safety. The Georgia Department of Natural Resources also provides extensive information on safety practices in motorized vessels, http://www.georgiawildlife.com/boating/safety.

ROCK ISLAND, REYNOLDS BEND, FLOYD COUNTY

## Know the River and Prepare for Your Trip

If you are reading this, you've taken the first step toward a safe river trip—know the section of river that you plan to travel, and understand its unique dangers. For example, the Etowah Falls section includes a Class IV rapid, and the Indian Mounds section includes a lowhead dam—never attempt to paddle over a lowhead dam. Do not attempt river sections that are beyond your skill levels. Leave your trip itinerary with someone else who can notify the authorities if you don't return as planned. Remember, what you take on the trip is all that you have to survive and rescue yourself. Carry appropriate food, water, clothes, and rescue equipment. While no section of the Etowah is more than a day's walk from "civilization," expect the unexpected and plan accordingly.

## Wear the Right Clothes

Wear the appropriate clothes to protect from sun, heat, rain, and cold. Cold water is especially dangerous, as extended contact with cold and wet can lead to hypothermia and even death. During cool weather, dress in layers using clothing made of synthetic fabrics such as polypropylene, nylon, neoprene, and polyester fleece. Always bring extra clothing protected in a waterproof container. When temperatures are below 60 degrees Fahrenheit or combined air and water temperatures are below 120 degrees Fahrenheit, wear a wet suit or dry suit. Waterproof shoes, socks, and gloves are also recommended. Always wear secure-fitting river shoes to protect your feet. Helmets should always be worn when paddling whitewater.

## Watch for Other Boaters

This safety practice is especially important on Lake Allatoona and on the white-water sections of the Etowah. Lake Allatoona experiences heavy motorized-boat traffic. Paddlers should stay close to shores and avoid main channels whenever possible. Waves created by motorboats are best navigated by turning the bow (nose) of the boat into the wave rather than taking the wave broadside. When paddling at night, a white light must be shown toward oncoming traffic. On the whitewater sections of the Etowah (and in other locations where navigational hazards exist), paddlers should confirm that downstream boaters are clear of the rapid or obstacle before proceeding.

### BOATER'S CHECKLIST

- ☐ A Spare Paddle . . . because paddles break and motors die
- ☐ Hat or Helmet . . . hat for sun protection and/or warmth and a helmet whenever paddling whitewater
- ☐ Whistle or Signaling Device . . . three sharp blows on a whistle are a universal distress signal
- ☐ Throw Bags (ropes) and Other Rescue Gear . . . especially important in whitewater
- ☐ "River" Knife . . . a safely and easily accessible knife can save a life entangled in rope or other hazards
- ☐ Bilge Pump or Bailer . . . because holes in boats do happen
- ☐ Extra Clothing in Dry Bag . . . dry clothes keep you warm; wet clothes, not so much.
- ☐ Sunscreen
- ☐ Compass and Map
- ☐ First-Aid Kit
- ☐ Matches
- ☐ Small Boat Repair Kit with Duct Tape

# Boating Etiquette
## Practice No-Trace Travel

Practicing no-trace travel is simple: just remember to leave your route so that those who come behind would never know that someone passed before them. Never litter and always pack out trash (including the trash of those less considerate).

Conduct all toilet activity at least 200 feet from any body of water. Bury your waste in a cathole 6–8 inches deep or pack it out. Be conscious of private property and do not conduct your toilet activity in someone's backyard.

ETOWAH, CHEROKEE COUNTY

Additionally . . .

- Avoid building campfires, except in established fire rings or in emergencies.
- Minimize impacts to shore when launching, portaging, scouting, or taking out.
- Examine, but do not touch, cultural or historic structures and artifacts.
- Leave rocks, plants, and other natural objects as you find them.
- Do not disturb wildlife.

## Respect Others

The Etowah is traveled by many, and many people make their homes along it. Always be respectful of other river users and riverfront property owners. Poor behavior by some river users can adversely impact other users through increased regulation and fees, limitations on access, and damage to the environment. The vast majority of property along the Etowah is privately owned. Islands within the river are also private property. While Georgia law allows boaters the right of passage on navigable streams, the law does not extend the right to travel on private property. Remain in the river channel, except in cases where you know public land exists or where you know that property owners allow boaters access.

Additionally . . .

- Know and obey all rules and regulations.
- Be courteous and polite when communicating with others.
- Avoid interfering with the recreational activities of others.
- Never engage in loud, lewd, or inappropriate behavior.
- Take care to avoid paddling near areas of heightened security (such as Allatoona Dam and some industrial facilities).
- Control pets or leave them at home.

## A Note on Parking at Launch Sites and Take Outs

While many popular launch and take out sites have designated parking areas or pull-offs on rights-of-way, some river access locations identified in this guide do not have adequate parking. Care should be taken when parking vehicles and unloading boats. Avoid parking on roadsides wherever possible.

## How to Use This Book

Each chapter presents a portion of the river that can generally be run within a single day and provides essential information about the estimated length of the run (both in hours and miles), the river level necessary to attempt the run, the location where the current level may be found, and directions to launch and take out sites. The largest portion of each chapter presents, by mile and GPS coordinate, points of interest one will find along the river. The map provided with each chapter is intended for use as a reference while on the river. For that reason, all the maps are oriented from upstream to downstream rather than from north to south and present only the most important roads for reference; it is assumed that drivers will use, in conjunction with the written directions to launch and take out sites, a road atlas or GPS system.

FISH WEIR, CHEROKEE COUNTY

# An Etowah River Fishing Primer

Spanning three distinct geographic regions, the Etowah's fishery is as diverse as the landscape surrounding it. With 75 native fish species, the Etowah has something to offer every angler.

## Trout Water
### (Headwaters, Hightower, Etowah Falls, and Tunneling for Gold maps)

The Etowah's rapids, runs, and waterfalls provide you with all you would expect from a mountain trout stream. Upstream of Hightower Church Road (Lower Crossing), the Etowah, and all of the tributaries are seasonal trout streams that are open from the last Saturday in March through October 31. The remainder of the river in Lumpkin County is open to fishing all year. Most of the river can be waded easily, and casting upstream is usually the best approach. Trout in Georgia are not necessarily the same finicky feeders as their cousins out west. Georgia trout will eat just about any fly, live or dead bait, or artificial lures. For fly casters, caddis and mayfly patterns as well as streamers produce well. If the water is dingy, fishing deep, slow, big, and gaudy is the way to go. If the water is running clear, small bright-colored flies cast to the shadows yield the best results.

STRIPED BASS FISHING ON ETOWAH, BARTOW COUNTY

Whether you use bait casting or spinning rod, employ stealth. Georgia trout are not selective, but they do spook easily. Always be careful to avoid moving overhead limbs or casting shadows across pools and runs. Getting the bait or lure into the water without alerting the fish is the only way to be successful.

## Sunfish of Dawson County
### (Big Savannah, Dawson Forest, and Eagle's Beak maps)

As the river flows out of Lumpkin County into Dawson County, the river begins its swing westward, and although a few trout are still to be found in the cooler months, water temperatures increase and the primary fish are sunfish. Sunfish are a diverse family, and the ones that occupy this part of the river are primarily redeye bass, rock bass, spotted bass, and cool-water bream varieties.

The fly angler can now switch to a heavier rod and larger flies. Popping bugs, leech patterns, and wooly buggers work great for the bass family and may even pick up an errant catfish. Because the green sunfish, red breast, long ear, and spotted sunfish have smaller mouths than the bass, you will have more success with them if you use smaller popping bugs, dry flies, and wet flies.

The best time to fish for sunfish is in warmer weather. In the cold months you might swear there are no fish at all in the river. They are there, just sluggish and harder to catch. Spinners such as Mepps, Panther Martin, and Blue Fox are perfect to attract any of the sunfish family. Small minnow-type lures, live minnows, and almost any live bait are good choices in the Dawson County section of the river.

## Migratory Sport Fish of Cherokee County
(McGraw Ford, Canton, and Lake Allatoona Backwaters maps)

After leaving Dawson County, the river slows and warms even more. Just as the river has changed, so have the fish species. Redeye bass have now almost disappeared, replaced by largemouth bass and spotted bass. Large blue cats and channel cats can be found, and since the river soon dumps into Lake Allatoona, migratory species begin to show themselves. White bass, striped bass, and crappie all swim upstream in the spring when the water temperatures are perfect for each species.

The white bass make their run up the river in late winter or early spring. If the dogwood trees are budding, the white bass are making their move. White bass will eat minnows, jigs, small crank baits, and spinners. Whites usually congregate at creek mouths and eddies associated with sandbars. Sometimes small striped bass can be found schooling with the whites, and these fish will hit the same baits.

SHOALS AT RAVENAL CAVE, BARTOW COUNTY

Striped bass usually make their spawning run a few weeks after the whites. Even though the current flow and temperature combination needed for a successful spawn does not exist in this part of the river, the stripers can still be found. These fish love live shad, large minnow lures, and big jigs. Heavier tackle is needed for stripers, as they range up to 30 pounds. In late summer as the lake begins to warm, they will return to the river seeking cooler water.

Catfish of all sizes are usually found in the deeper, slow sections of the river near Canton. Chicken livers, night crawlers, shad, and cut baits fished on the bottom are the best bets for the cat family. The larger the bait, the larger the fish you might catch. Thirty-pound cats are caught every year by the patient bait fisherman.

## Lake Allatoona
### (Lake Allatoona Backwaters and Lake Allatoona maps)

Lake Allatoona is home to a variety of sport fish. During the summer, heavy recreational boat traffic makes portions of the lake almost unfishable during the daylight hours, but night fishing with minnows for crappie under lights can be very rewarding. All members of the bass family can be landed on the lake. Stripers and hybrids can be caught using the large minnow lures, shad, or small trout, or by trolling.

Sometimes the lake will have a turnover in the spring and fall. In the fall, this is when the lake surface begins to cool and this water becomes heavier. Often the surface water sinks to the bottom and the oxygen-deprived bottom water rises. The effect often results in a die-off of the shad. When stripers and hybrids gather to feed on the dead and dying shad, fishing can be very productive.

VIEW FROM RAVENAL CAVE, BARTOW COUNTY

Allatoona has many narrow coves that are not conducive to water-skiers and personal water craft. These coves give the largemouth bass protected places for their spawning beds. Soft baits, such as plastic worms, lizards, and jigs, can yield a trophy-sized bass or a bunch of good, eating-sized fish. During the colder months daylight fishing is much easier and almost any fish can be caught on points and sandbars.

## Tailwater Fishing
### (Indian Mounds, Euharlee, Hardin Bridge, Reynolds Bend, and Rome maps)

Because of the operation of Allatoona Dam, the Etowah in Bartow and Floyd counties has two distinct personalities: generation flow and nongeneration flow at normal low water. Boaters and wade anglers should always be aware of the power generation schedule at Allatoona Dam before embarking on a trip; call (706) 334-7213 for release schedule. Failure to understand this schedule and to heed the signs of rising water can result in the loss of property and life.

FISH WEIR ADJACENT TO ETOWAH INDIAN MOUNDS, BARTOW COUNTY

The river here is characterized by long pools that vary from waist deep to 10 feet or more, and these sections offer the angler the opportunity to fish the logs and rock outcrops for spotted bass and bream. Lures and flies work as well as anything. The same pools offer some great bottom-fishing. The river is full of catfish, drum, smallmouth buffalo, Asian carp, and grass carp. Night crawlers work best for the small cats and the rest of the group, except the grass carp. The big cats will hit large-cut bait such as shad or bream. If you see evidence of grass carp, a dough ball mixed with corn floating on the surface works well. Sometimes wild grapes floating on the surface in the fall will get a fish, especially if there are muscadine vines dropping the grapes into the river. Be sure to use heavy tackle, because these fish grow to 100 pounds.

Striped bass are caught with regularity from midspring into early fall on the same baits and lures mentioned earlier. Stripers come up the river from the Coosa and Oostanaula Rivers. By late May they can be caught anywhere in the river from Thompson Weinman Dam downstream to Rome. At low levels the Etowah has perfect wading areas for catching striped bass. There are stretches of the river that are

knee to waist deep for 1 mile or more. These shallow areas often have one or more fish weirs crossing them. These weirs act as funnels that the stripers often use to their advantage. The stripers wait in an eddy on the downstream side of the funnel mouth and ambush a shad or other baitfish as the baitfish swims downstream. An angler should either wade or position the boat 50 feet or so below the mouth of the weir, out of the current, and cast the lure to the upstream side of the funnel. Then the retrieve should be fast enough to surpass the speed of the current so that the bait has a natural action. If a striper is there, be prepared to wind faster and set the hook hard. If you happen to be at this type of spot as the generation flow is making the water rise, the fishing can be fantastic. This is when being in a boat or canoe is imperative for safety's sake.

A word of caution about fish caught in the Etowah: the Georgia Department of Natural Resources issues fish consumption guidelines for specific species caught in various sections of the Etowah from Dawson County to Floyd County due to elevated levels of mercury and PCBs, contaminants that can cause a variety of health problems in humans who consume these fish. Generally, the largest predatory fish contain the highest levels of contaminants. Smaller fish are safer to eat. Consult the Fish Consumption Guidelines at the Department of Natural Resources website: http://gaepd.org/Documents/fish_guide.html

Compiled by PAUL DIPRIMA

Coosa Valley Chapter Trout Unlimited

# Headwaters

**Length** 7 miles (Hightower Gap to Hightower Church Road)

**Class** This section is accessed by foot travel only; however, the section from the upper crossing of Hightower Church Road to the lower crossing of Hightower Church Road (2.2 miles) can be floated during periods of sufficient flow.

**Time** 4–8 hours on foot

**Minimum Level** Levels of 200 cubic feet per second or greater at the U.S. Geological Survey gauge at Ga. 9 west of Dahlonega are recommended for the 2-mile run between the upper and lower crossings of Hightower Church Road. Rapids in this section do not exceed Class I in difficulty. A quick look at the shoals at the upper crossing of Hightower Church Road will indicate if water levels are sufficient. Sections above this road crossing include significant waterfalls and are not recommended for paddling.

---

**River Gauge** The nearest river gauge is located at Ga. 9 downstream from the launch site: http://waterdata.usgs.gov/ga/nwis/uv?site_no=02388900.

**Trailhead** The trailhead for this section is located off Forest Service (FS) Road 42 where the Appalachian Trail passes through Hightower Gap. Parking is available where FS Road 42 and FS Road 69 intersect at Hightower Gap.

DIRECTIONS The trailhead is located at the intersection of FS Road 42 and FS Road 69. From the intersection of U.S. 19 and Ga. 52 in Dahlonega, travel north on Ga. 52 (S. Chestatee St.) to Dahlonega Square. At the square, bear right and continue straight on Main Street for 0.1 mile to Ga. 60 (N. Grove St.). Turn left onto Ga. 60 and proceed 2.3 miles to Camp Wahsega Road on the left. Turn left and proceed 8.4 miles to the intersection with Cooper Gap Road / Hightower Church Road at the entrance to Camp Frank D. Merrill. Turn right onto Cooper Gap Road and proceed 2.8 miles to the top of the ridge and the intersection with FS Road 42. Turn left onto FS Road 42 and proceed 3.7 miles to the intersection with FS Road 69. The parking area is on the right.

**Hightower Church Road Launch Site** The launch site is located where Hightower Church Road crosses the Etowah at a Forest Service campground 0.7 mile south of the Camp Wahsega 4-H Center. There is no developed boat launch at this location.

DIRECTIONS Follow the trailhead directions above to the intersection of Camp Wahsega Road and Cooper Gap Road / Hightower Church Road at the entrance to Camp Merrill. Turn left onto Hightower Church Road and proceed 1.6 miles to the Etowah River.

Trail's End / Take Out Site  The take out for this section is located beneath the bridge at the lower crossing of Hightower Church Road. Chattahoochee National Forest property is located downstream from the bridge and a pull-off at the intersection of Miles Berry Road and Hightower Church Road just east of the river provides vehicle access. Property upstream from Hightower Church Road is private.

Description  This is the birthplace of the Etowah. In its 7-mile run from Hightower Gap to Hightower Church Road, the Etowah descends more than 1,400 feet and cascades over numerous waterfalls, culminating in the 60-foot Black Falls. The scenery is wild with the notable exception of the river's course through the heart of Camp Frank D. Merrill, a U.S. Army Ranger training station. After passing through the camp, the river continues its wild, twisting journey, finally becoming a navigable river at its first crossing of Hightower Church Road. Unmarked trails follow the river's course from Hightower Gap to the lower crossing of Hightower Road. Though most of the treadway is well worn, some portions require improvisation and bushwhacking.

Outfitters  Appalachian Outfitters in Dahlonega is the nearest canoe and kayak outfitter.

## Points of Interest

(34.663250, -84.129933) Hightower Gap & Appalachian Trail. Hightower Gap marks the Tennessee Valley Divide and a dip along the Appalachian Trail. As such, it is the launch site of many a long journey. On the northwest side of this ridge, rain flows downhill to Rock Creek and from there to the Toccoa River and Lake Blue Ridge, then on to the Ocoee River in Tennessee, the Hiawassee, the Tennessee, the Ohio, the Mississippi, and finally into the Gulf of Mexico—a journey of nearly 2,000 miles. Rain falling on the Etowah side of the ridge takes a less circuitous route to the sea. It flows down the Etowah to Rome and on to the Coosa and Alabama Rivers before reaching Mobile Bay—a journey of about 760 miles, yet Mobile Bay and the mouth of the Mississippi are separated by only 100 miles. From Hightower Gap, it's an 8-mile hike to the southern terminus of the Appalachian Trail at Springer Mountain and a 2,172-mile hike to the northern terminus at Mount Katahdin in Maine.

CAMP MERRILL WATER INTAKE, LUMPKIN COUNTY

HEADWATERS, LUMPKIN COUNTY

MILE 0 (34.662544, -84.129017) Etowah Spring. A trail from Hightower Gap leads down to the spring that is considered the source of the Etowah. This trail continues to parallel the river on its course from Hightower Gap to Camp Frank D. Merrill. Hikers can follow this trail or simply follow the path of the river itself. From the spring to Camp Merrill Road, the river descends over numerous cascades and passes beneath a mix of hardwood and hemlock forests.

MILE 0.9 (34.651533, -84.120458) Camp Merrill Road. A dirt road leads from this spot downstream to Camp Merrill, providing vehicle access through the Ranger camp into the Etowah's headwaters.

MILE 2.4 (34.634450, -84.108314) Camp Frank D. Merrill. Evidence of the Ranger camp can be seen well before reaching the main base, as the army uses the Etowah's headwaters for many training exercises, but at 2.5 miles from Hightower Gap, a large clearing on river right marks the beginning of the base's facilities that straddle the Etowah for the next mile. The army allows the public access to the camp, but be considerate of the soldiers engaged in training exercises. Just downstream from the clearing is an intake structure that supplies the base with its drinking water (the first human utilization of the river). Ranger training in the area dates back to the early 1950s, with the army moving to this location in 1960. At this facility army Rangers endure a training course that prepares them for combat in mountainous terrain. The schooling includes a requirement to complete a 200-foot night-time rappel. Camp Merrill is named in honor of General Dow Merrill, leader of the legendary Merrill's Marauders who fought against the Japanese in World War II in Burma. His unit began their 1944 Burma campaign 3,000 strong, but after five months of battle in the jungle, the group was reduced by casualties, combat injuries, and illness to a fighting

HEADWATERS, LUMPKIN COUNTY

force of 130. Nevertheless, the team marched some 1,000 miles and captured a key Japanese airfield—a feat unsurpassed by any other U.S. fighting force in World War II.

MILE 2.9 (34.627375, -84.105878) Ranger Memorial. Adjacent to the Mosby Heliport at the camp is a small kiosk paying tribute to army Rangers who have fallen in service to their country. In this area you'll also find training structures used to simulate helicopters and transport planes.

MILE 3.2 (34.623433, -84.106028) Black Falls. This 60-foot waterfall is situated in the heart of the Ranger training area. At the base of the falls is a former rock quarry that is now used by the Rangers for climbing and rappelling exercises. A rugged trail leads along the bank on river right.

MILE 3.5 (34.620014, -84.105756) Lower Black Falls. Located just downstream from a small dam used to flood bottomlands for Ranger training, this cascade spills about 20 feet into a beautiful swimming hole.

MILE 4.7 (34.608375, -84.096806) Hightower Church Road & Camp Wahsega (Upper Crossing). A primitive forest service campground is located along the river upstream from the road here. Following Hightower Church Road to the north brings you to Camp Wahsega, a 4-H camp with a storied history. In 1933 a Civilian Conservation Corps camp was established at the site to employ local men, including many out-of-work and disabled World War I veterans. Crews from Camp C-11 crushed rock from the quarry (visible just below Black Falls), built and improved roads, fought forest fires, and constructed some of the nearby recreational reservoirs, including Lake Winfield Scott near Suches and Lake Trahlyta in Vogel State Park. The men worked for $30 per month, $25 of which was sent to their families. In the late 1930s the facility became a 4-H camp and remains so today. The University of Georgia Cooperative Extension Service conducts environmental and outdoor education for youth from across the state.

MILE 6.2 (34.599086, -84.081372) River Cane. Growing in dense stands bordering the river as it winds through pastureland here, river cane is among the Etowah's most common riparian plants, yet this large stand would pale in comparison to the canebrakes one might have seen here in the 1700s. Botanist William Bartram described canebrakes "rolling to the horizon like an ocean." In fact, scientists estimate that river cane has been eliminated from 95 percent of its original habitat. Canebrakes like this one provide habitat and food for wildlife and help stabilize riverbanks. Their destruction has likely contributed to the pollution of our streams, as they also play a critical role in slowing stormwater and filtering pollutants. For Native Americans, river cane was a critical raw material. They used it for nearly everything, fashioning it into spears, arrows, baskets, homes, mats, knives, torches, rafts, tubes, and drills. River cane propagates primarily through rhizomes, with these spreading roots leading to the dense clusters of plants found in canebrakes. However, river cane is not so effective propagating through its seeds. River cane flowers sporadically (every 30 to 40 years), and its seeds have a low germination rate. The canebrakes also lend their name to the canebrake rattlesnake because this venomous snake is commonly found along the borders of swamps and wetlands—also the preferred habitat of river cane.

MILE 6.9 (34.593247, -84.077931) Hightower Church Road (Lower Crossing).

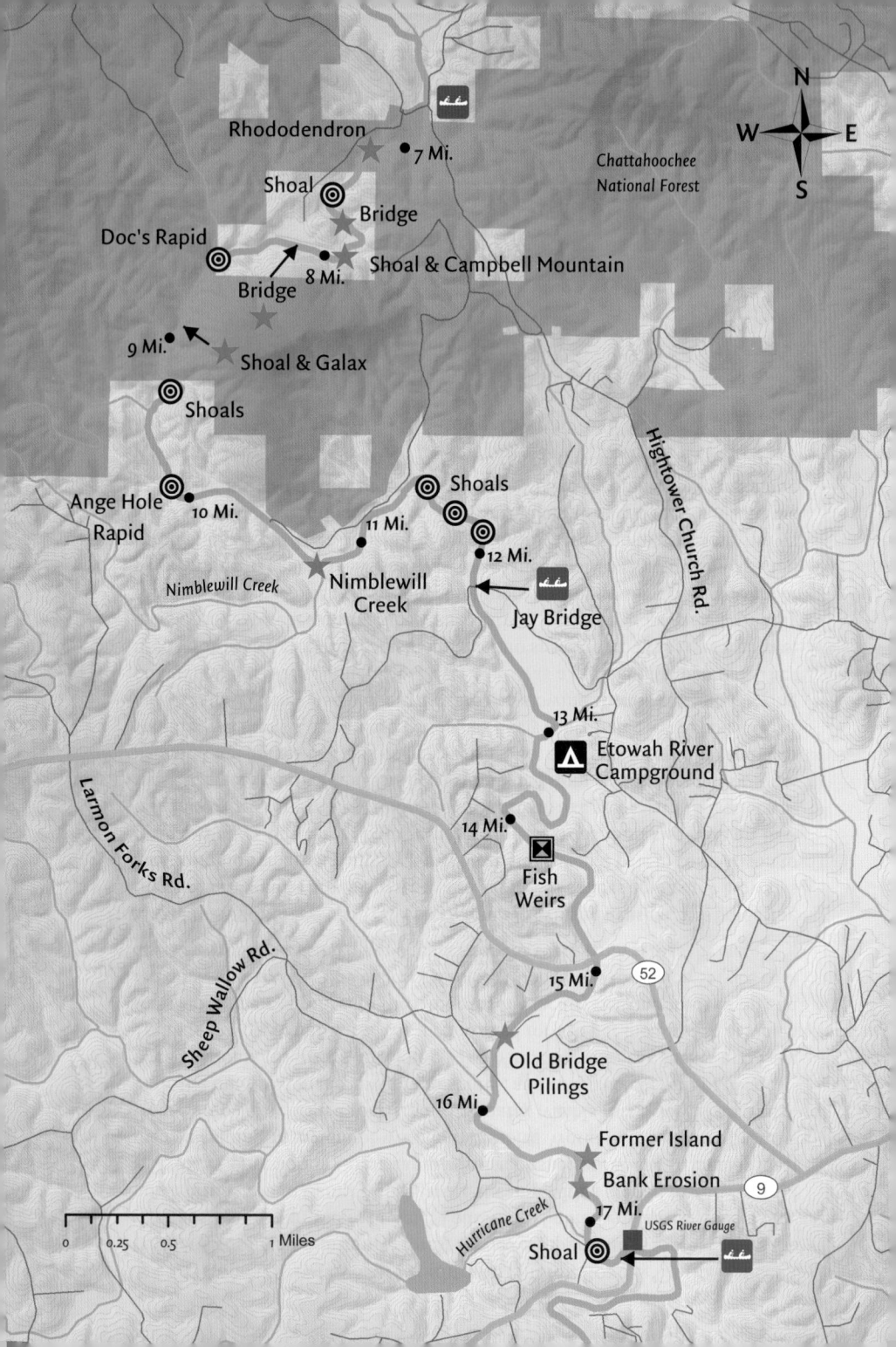

# Hightower

**Length** 11 miles (Hightower Church Road to Ga. 9)

**Class** I–II

**Time** 5–8 hours

**Minimum Level** This section includes numerous shoals that require sufficient flows to navigate. Levels of 200 cubic feet per second (cfs) or greater at the U.S. Geological Survey gauge at Ga. 9 west of Dahlonega are recommended for the run from Hightower Church Road to Jay Bridge. The section can be run at lower levels—just be prepared to portage around several shoals and ledges for lack of water. Below Jay Bridge, flows as low as 70 cfs are adequate for the run to Ga. 9.

ANGE HOLE RAPID, LUMPKIN COUNTY

**River Gauge** The nearest river gauge is located at Ga. 9 downstream from the launch site: http://waterdata.usgs.gov/ga/nwis/uv?site_no=02388900.

**Launch Site** There is no developed launch at this site. However, a pull-off on the left side of Hightower Church Road prior to its intersection with Miles Berry Road provides access to the river from Chattahoochee National Forest property. Property upstream of the bridge is private. A steep slide leads to the river beneath the bridge.

DIRECTIONS The launch is located at the intersection of Hightower Church Road and Miles Berry Road north of Ga. 52 west of Dahlonega. From the intersection of U.S. 19 and Ga. 52 in Dahlonega, travel west on Ga. 52 3.9 miles to Siloam Church Road on the right. Turn right and proceed 2.9 miles to the intersection with Jay Bridge Road. Continue straight on Hightower Church Road 3 miles to Miles Berry Road. A gravel turnoff just before one reaches Miles Berry Road provides access to the river just downstream from the Hightower Church Road Bridge.

**Take Out Site** The take out is located on river right just upstream from Ga. 9. There is no developed launch here, and the take out requires a steep haul. A parking area is beneath the bridge.

DIRECTIONS From the launch site, return to Ga. 52 via Hightower Church Road and Siloam Church Road. At Ga. 52, turn right and proceed 0.5 mile to the intersection of Ga. 9 and Ga. 52. Bear left on Ga. 9 and proceed 1.6 miles to the Etowah River. Cross the bridge and turn right into the gravel drive leading to the parking area beneath the bridge.

Description Mountain streams don't get much more intimate. For the first 5 miles the tiny Etowah winds through tunnels of rhododendron as it makes its way around Campbell Mountain, flowing over two Class II shoals before slowing and opening up below Jay Bridge. From there, it winds through bottomlands, where evidence of hundreds of years of human habitation reveals itself in the uppermost fish weirs on the Etowah.

Outfitters Water levels permitting, Appalachian Outfitters in Dahlonega runs canoe and kayak rentals and shuttle service on this section of river.

## Points of Interest

MILE 7.2 (34.590094, -84.082417) Rhododendron. Below Hightower Church Road and around the flanks of Campbell Mountain, rhododendron arches over the river, in places forming enchanting tunnels. The species here is *Rhododendron maximum*, commonly called great laurel. A resident of stream banks throughout

the southern Appalachians, great laurel blooms midsummer and keeps its glossy leaves year round. The name comes from the Greek *rhodo*, meaning "rose," and *dendron*, meaning "tree."

**MILE 7.6** (34.586600, -84.086036) Shoal.

**MILE 7.7** (34.585431, -84.085094) Bridge. This low bridge requires a limbo in high water and should be approached with caution. Strainers also often clog the river as the bridge and pilings catch logs and other debris.

**MILE 7.9** (34.582819, -84.084597) Shoal & Campbell Mountain. At this bend, the Etowah slams against the north flank of Campbell Mountain. From here to the 2,053-foot summit, it's a 1,000-foot climb. The Etowah loops around the base of the mountain for the next 4 miles.

**MILE 8.1** (34.583497, -84.088189) Bridge.

**MILE 8.6** (34.582494, -84.095286) Doc's Rapid. A short series of small shoals leads to this cross-river ledge that creates a borderline Class II rapid with a 2-foot drop. A pool below the ledge provides easy recovery.

UPSTREAM OF HIGHTOWER CHURCH ROAD
LOWER CROSSING, LUMPKIN COUNTY

MILE 8.9 (34.577539, -84.098739)
Shoal & Galax. The ground
cover along the riverbanks here,
with deep green, tooth-edged,
round, heart-shaped leaves, is
known as galax. During the
winter, some leaves of this
perennial evergreen turn bronze
or dull crimson. In the spring
galax sends up long, thin stalks,
and later in the summer these
stalks sport a cluster of tiny
white flowers. Because of the
leaves' beauty—and the fact that
the plant holds its color for so
long—galax has traditionally
been harvested for use by commercial florists. Overharvesting
led the U.S. Forest Service, in
2005, to restrict collections to
May and June, when new leaves
emerge.

DOC'S RAPID, LUMPKIN COUNTY

MILE 9.4 (34.573494, -84.099350) Shoals.

MILE 9.9 (34.566450, -84.098100) Ange Hole Rapid. This wide sliding drop of about 6 feet creates a Class II rapid. A large pool at the base of this fall provides easy recovery.

MILE 10.7 (34.561667, -84.086997) Nimblewill Creek. On river right is Nimblewill Creek, a tributary that in the 1800s fed a hardscrabble mountain community with the same unique name. Descendents of the area's first settlers recount that the community's moniker derived from the residents' common "will" that the place be growing and active—or nimble, if you will. Of course, Nimblewill is also the name of native turfgrass common to the Southeast. Life in the 1800s in Nimblewill was tough, in fact, too tough for many. The wife of one early settler left her husband, who had brought her to the place. In divorce papers she claimed that Nimblewill was "not a place fit to live" and that the roads were so bad that she often couldn't make it to church. She returned to more civilized Gainesville. But Nimblewill's greatest contribution to the area is probably a 33-mile-long ditch, or aqueduct, that carried water from this mountain stream to the Kin Mori gold mine south of Dawsonville. Mining engineers needed water sources from higher elevations to maintain enough pressure to blast away topsoil in the hydraulic mining process—thus the ambitious undertaking.

MILE 11.4 (34.566972, -84.077642) Shoals.

MILE 11.7 (34.565208, -84.075278) Shoals. This marks the beginning of a 0.1-mile series of small shoals that culminates in a 3-foot slide.

MILE 11.9 (34.563369, -84.072900) Shoals. Another 0.1-mile stretch of continuous swift water.

MILE 12.2 (34.560225, -84.074256) Jay Bridge. In the mid-1870s Vermont emigrant Frank W. Hall harnessed the power of the Etowah here to establish a sawmill and gristmill. Later he added a tannery to his business portfolio, along with a store and a post office. The village that grew up around the mill became known as Jay and thrived through the 1880s and 1890s, but by 1923, the *Dahlonega Nugget* reported that "there is nothing there to mark the once very busy place." Hall went on to become Dahlonega's mayor and represented the area in the Georgia legislature. A story is told that while digging the foundation for his home near the Dahlonega Square, he found a vein of gold. City leaders denied him the opportunity to mine the vein, for they didn't want a mining mess on the town square. Hall, who had other properties on the square, agreed and proceeded to build his house atop the gold. He died in 1901.

MILE 13.3 (34.547606, -84.067981) Etowah River Campground. This private campground of 28 acres hugs the east bank of the river for some 1,800 feet. The campground offers RV and tent camping, a bathhouse with hot showers, and laundry facilities. During trout season, the riverbanks are busy with fishermen.

MILE 14.2 (34.542275, -84.067922) Fish Weirs. Along this straightaway are two V-shaped rock dams that are likely the uppermost Native American fish weirs on the Etowah. From here to Rome, dozens of these rock structures cross the river. Built by Native Americans 500 to 1,000 years ago (and in many cases maintained and improved by subsequent residents), the weirs, or traps, were used to catch fish by corralling them to the point of the V, where they could be scuttled into a basket.

MILE 15.5 (34.529550, -84.070989) Old Bridge Pilings.

MILE 16.7 (34.521006, -84.064383) Former Island. On river left here, the Etowah once split its flow around a large island. Now, the full flow stays in the main channel, though dated maps still show a distinctive isle.

MILE 16.8 (34.519953, -84.064431) Bank Erosion. Here the Etowah does what rivers do best—carve new courses through the process of erosion and deposition. And they tend to take anything perched on those threatened banks downstream with them. Beneath this eroded bank and downstream you'll find farm debris that at one time was high and dry.

MILE 17.2 (34.514822, -84.063239) Shoal.

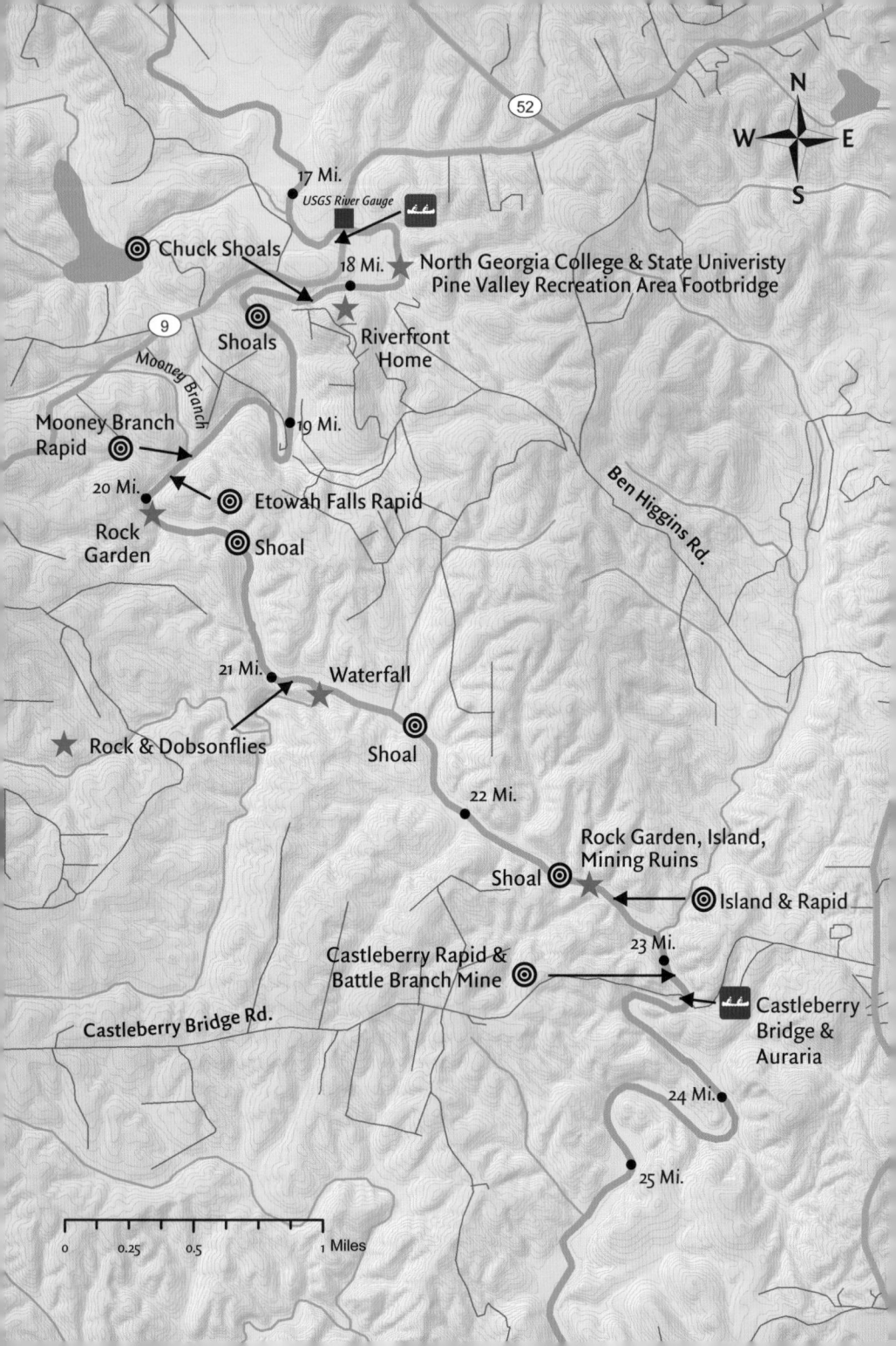

# Etowah Falls

Length  6 miles (Ga. 9 to Castleberry Bridge Road)

Class  I–IV

Time  3–6 hours

Minimum Level  This section includes numerous shoals that require sufficient flows to navigate. Levels of 100 cubic feet per second (cfs) or greater at the U.S. Geological Survey gauge at Ga. 9 west of Dahlonega should provide sufficient flow. Below 100 cfs, it is still runnable, but be prepared to do some walking. In flows above 300 cfs, paddlers should use caution when approaching Etowah Falls.

River Gauge  The nearest river gauge is located at the Ga. 9 launch site: http://waterdata.usgs.gov/ga/nwis/uv?site_no=02388900.

Launch Site  There is no developed boat launch at this site, and the descent to the river is steep. However, there is ample parking beneath the Ga. 9 bridge. A gravel drive on the south side of the river and west side of the road leads to the parking area and launch site beneath the bridge.

DIRECTIONS  The launch is located on Ga. 9 north of Dawsonville. From the intersection of Ga. 400 and Ga. 136 north of Dawsonville, go west on Ga. 136 and proceed 6 miles. Turn right onto Ga. 9 and proceed 7 miles to the gravel road on the left prior to crossing the river. Parking is beneath the bridge and in an open area adjacent to bridge.

SHOALS NEAR CASTLEBERRY BRIDGE, LUMPKIN COUNTY

Take Out Site  The take out is located on river right just above Castleberry Bridge (and just below Castleberry Rapid). There is no developed boat launch at this site, but rock outcroppings provide a suitable take out with a moderate descent to the river. Parking areas are located on both sides of Castleberry Bridge Road on the west side of the river.

DIRECTIONS  From the Ga. 9 parking area, return to Ga. 9. Turn right and proceed 4.8 miles. Turn left onto Castleberry Bridge Road and proceed 3 miles to the parking areas on either side of the road before reaching the bridge.

Description  The most popular whitewater run on the Etowah and the birthplace of North America's first gold rush, this 6-mile section provides three Class II rapids and one Class IV rapid (if you're inclined to run Etowah Falls). It also provides breathtaking scenery, interrupted occasionally by riverfront homes, some of which crowd the riverbanks. Based on today's scenery, it's hard to believe that this part of the river was crawling with gold prospectors in the 1830s.

Outfitters  Water levels permitting, Appalachian Outfitters in Dahlonega runs canoe and kayak rentals and shuttle service on this section of river.

## Points of Interest

MILE 17.7 (34.512619, -84.056464) North Georgia College & State University Pine Valley Recreation Area Footbridge. From Ga. 9 the Etowah winds 0.75 mile around this outdoor recreation facility operated by the state college in near-

ETOWAH FALLS, LUMPKIN COUNTY

by Dahlonega. The complex includes a recreation field, pavilion, sand volleyball court, and ropes course that can be rented by the public. It was originally used as an army training camp.

MILE 18.1 (34.511656, -84.060675) Riverfront Home. This home is one of several that crowd the banks through this 6-mile run. Although this home is grandfathered, structures can no longer be built this close to the water under current state law. Since 1989, Georgia law requires that a 25-foot vegetative buffer be maintained along all streams and rivers. On trout streams like this section of the Etowah, a 50-foot buffer is required. These buffers help prevent pollutants from entering streams, provide wildlife habitat, and of course, they protect the viewshed along rivers. However, regulating land use is not without controversy—Georgia's law governing erosion, sedimentation, and stream buffers has been amended more than a dozen times since its adoption in 1975. In many cases, these amendments have weakened the law, including a 2003 change that reduced the trout stream buffer from 100 feet.

SHOALS NEAR CASTLEBERRY BRIDGE, LUMPKIN COUNTY

MILE 18.3 (34.511094, -84.062578) Chuck Shoals. The best route through this Class II rapid starts on the left and ends in descent through the center chute. The rapid can be portaged, but be considerate of private property and do not linger on land.

MILE 18.5 (34.510250, -84.066292) Shoals. The next 0.2 mile provides a steady diet of swift-moving water over shallow shoals.

MILE 19.7 (34.510250, -84.066292) Mooney Branch Rapid. This ledge marks the beginning of the shoals leading up to Etowah Falls. The best routes through the ledge are down the middle or on far river left, with a sharp turn to the middle of the river. A long pool allows for recovery before the main shoals above Etowah Falls. Mooney Branch enters the river at the base of the rapid on river right.

MILE 19.8 (34.501497, -84.072181) Etowah Falls Rapid. A pair of ledges that add up to a Class II rapid lead to the main falls. A course down the middle takes you over these ledges to a small pool above the falls. After navigating the upper ledges, experienced boaters can find a line over the falls given adequate flows (above 80 cubic feet per second at the Ga. 9 gauge). Scouting is recommended! Boaters unable to navigate an eddy turn at the base of the second ledge directly above the falls should opt to portage on river right before entering the ledges. Otherwise, an unplanned journey over the falls may result. This is truly one of the most breathtaking spots on the Etowah. Rocks at the top of the falls make a nice respite. Below the main falls, the river descends over two smaller ledges. Portaging to the base of the falls provides access to these additional challenges.

MILE 20.1 (34.499311, -84.073225) Rock Garden. Around the bend from Etowah Falls is a rock garden that provides a swiftwater obstacle course.

MILE 20.5 (34.497706, -84.067428) Shoal.

MILE 21.1 (34.490147, -84.064011) Rock & Dobsonflies. The impressive rock outcropping on river right is also a breeding ground for dobsonflies, a common aquatic insect. The white splotches you might see on these rocks are their egg casings. After mating, the adult female lays 100–1,000 eggs on rocks or leaves overhanging the river and covers them with a white film that resembles bird droppings. Young dobsonflies emerge in their larval state known as hellgrammites and crawl or fall to the river. For the next two to three years, the young hellgrammites live under rocks in the stream, eating other aquatic insects and trying not to get eaten themselves. As the name suggests, these aquatic macroinvertebrates look rather hellish, with long, flat—but meaty—bodies and a scary set of jaws. Upon reaching maturity, hellgrammites crawl out of the water, form a cocoon on a rock or log, overwinter as a pupa, emerge the following summer as adults, fly about for a few days, mate, lay their eggs, and then die.

MILE 21.2 (34.489989, -84.062147) Waterfall. On river right here is an unnamed tributary that spills into the river over a short shoal. The splash of the falls is amplified by the grotto-like bowl formed by the creek's high banks and the wide pool beneath the falls.

MILE 21.5 (34.487697, -84.055594) Shoal.

MILE 22.4 (34.479233, -84.045250) Shoal.

MILE 22.5 (34.479306, -84.043758) Rock Garden, Island, Mining Ruins. After passing the large house on river left, the river descends, over the next 0.1 mile, into a dense rock garden with numerous shoals and rapids. On river right near the island are the remains of a gold-mining operation. The intensity of mining operations along the Etowah from 1828 until after the turn of the century is hard to fathom. Within two years after the first discovery of gold, Auraria (derived from the Latin word for gold—aurum), just to the east of this spot, was a thriving town of 1,000 residents. The first prospectors used only shovel and pan, but the impact on the local landscape was extreme. A traveler during the 1850s noted: "The beds of the creeks and brooks have been dug up, and the water now runs among unsightly heaps of gravel or through irregular pits." As the gold became harder to find, more-advanced techniques were employed, culminating in "hydraulic mining" in the late 1800s, in which pressurized water was used to literally wash away vast amounts of soil on the sides of hills and ridges to retrieve the gold.

MILE 22.6 (34.478414, -84.042244) Island & Rapid. This island marks the beginning of a 0.2-mile-long series of shoals and ledges that creates a challenging run. The best route is river right around the island, then angling back toward the middle of the river to ride the main flow over a series of ledges.

MILE 23.1 (34.473950, -84.037958) Castleberry Rapid & Battle Branch Mine. In low to normal flows, the best course through this Class II rapid is down the middle and then left of the large boulder on river left at the base of the run. On river right above Castleberry Rapid are the remains of the Battle Branch Mine. The mine earned its name when miners from Tennessee and Georgia in 1831 began arguing over possession of the claim. The fight that ensued left several of them seriously injured. Later, operations at the site were expanded by other gold seekers. At the height of excavation in 1878 the miners employed the hydraulic method, stripping the land bare with pressurized water and sending the ore to a stamp mill located on the river. Stamp mills were used to crush the ore into fine grains that could be sluiced, allowing the gold to be separated. Remains of the operation can still be seen.

MILE 23.2 (34.472697, -84.036875) Castleberry Bridge & Auraria. Castleberry Bridge Road is named for Elisha Castleberry, who, during Georgia's lotteries of former Cherokee lands in the 1830s, drew a land lot here. Castleberry was one of the early settlers of Auraria, located a mile east of the bridge. A town with a colorful mining history, Auraria actually gave birth to an entire state thanks to the Russell family, who, like Castleberry, were early settlers of the town. When the gold played out in Georgia, the Russells headed west, first to California and later to present-day Colorado, where in 1858 the eldest of the Russell men, Green Russell, discovered gold in Cherry Creek. Word quickly spread, and soon thereafter the town of Auraria (named in honor of the Georgia homeplace) sprang up. By 1860 the town of Auraria merged with nearby Denver, and thus Colorado became settled during the country's third gold rush—following Georgia in 1828 and California in 1849.

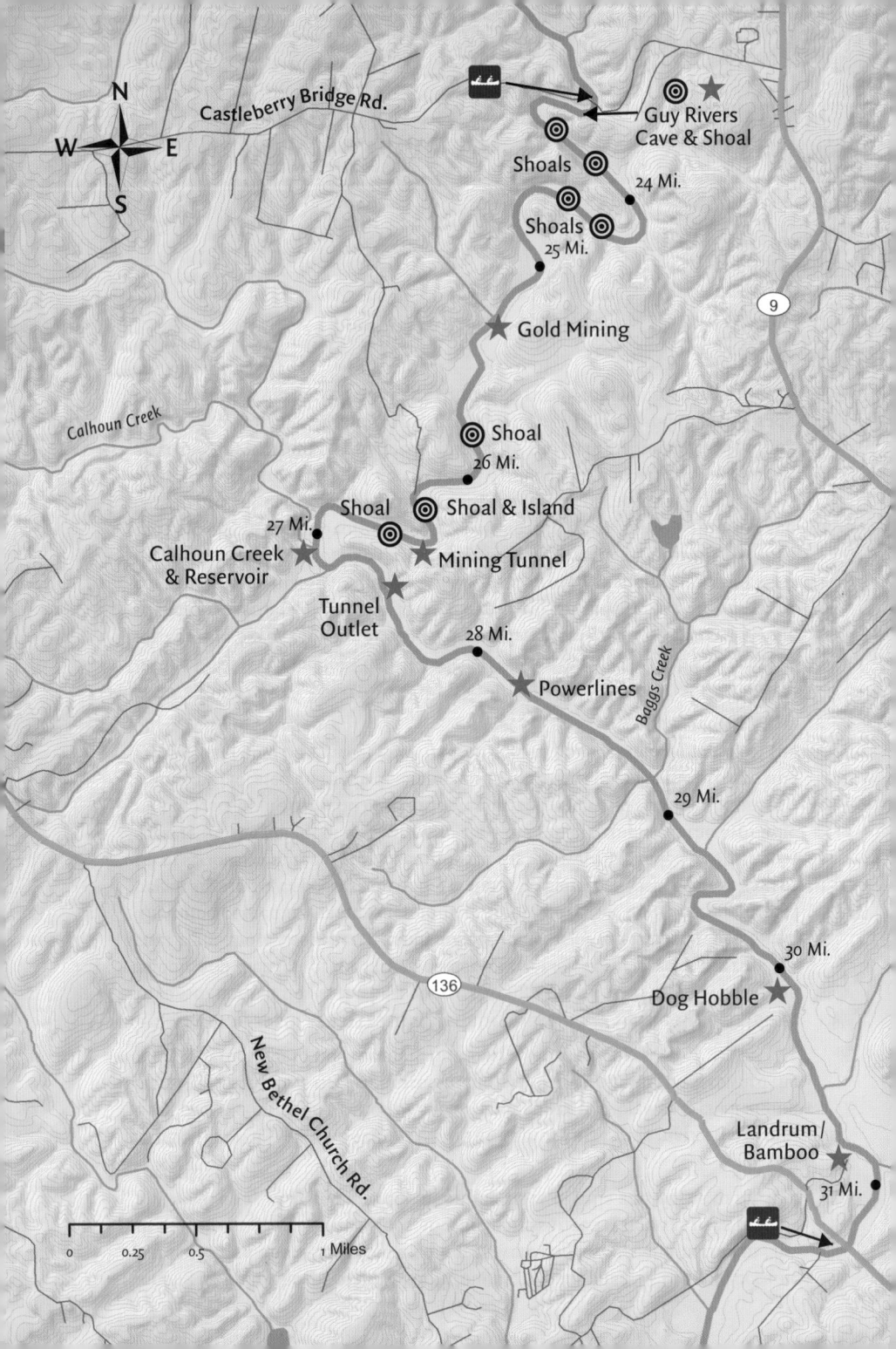

Castleberry Bridge Rd.

N
W · E
S

Guy Rivers
Cave & Shoal

Shoals

24 Mi.

Shoals

25 Mi.

Gold Mining

Calhoun Creek

Shoal

26 Mi.

Shoal

Shoal & Island

27 Mi.

Calhoun Creek
& Reservoir

Mining Tunnel

Tunnel
Outlet

28 Mi.

Powerlines

Baggs Creek

29 Mi.

30 Mi.

136

Dog Hobble

New Bethel Church Rd.

Landrum/
Bamboo

31 Mi.

9

0    0.25    0.5    1 Miles

# Tunneling for Gold

**Length** 8 miles (Castleberry Bridge Road to Ga. 136)

**Class** I–II

**Time** 3–6 hours

**Minimum Level** This section includes numerous shoals that require sufficient flows to navigate. Levels of 100 cubic feet per second or greater at the U.S. Geological Survey gauge at Ga. 9 west of Dahlonega should provide sufficient flow. Below 100 cubic feet per second, expect to do some walking.

---

**River Gauge** The nearest river gauge is located at Ga. 9 west of Dahlonega upstream from Castleberry Bridge: http://waterdata.usgs.gov/ga/nwis/uv?site_no=02388900.

**Launch Site** There is no developed boat launch at this site. Pull-offs on the north and south sides of the highway just west of the river provide limited parking. The launch site is upstream of the bridge and requires a short carry to the water's edge.

DIRECTIONS The launch is located on Castleberry Bridge Road north of Dawsonville. From the intersection of Ga. 400 and Ga. 136 north of Dawsonville, go west on Ga. 136 and proceed 0.1 mile to Auraria Road on the right. Turn right and proceed 6.6 miles. Turn left onto Castleberry Bridge Road and proceed 1 mile to the Etowah River. The pull-off is after the bridge.

DOWNSTREAM OF CASTLEBERRY BRIDGE, LUMPKIN COUNTY

**Take Out Site** The take out is located on river right below the Hwy. 136 bridge. There is no developed boat launch or parking area at this site. The parking area on the side of Ga. 136 is 0.1 mile from the river.

DIRECTIONS From the Castleberry Bridge Road parking area, return to Auraria Road. Turn right and proceed 6.6 miles. Turn right onto Ga. 136 and proceed 0.9 mile to the parking area on the right side of the highway west of the bridge.

Descriptions This 8-mile section runs through the heart of the area's historical gold mining region. Frequent shoals, Class I and borderline Class II, highlight the first 3 miles of the run, but this section is best known for the 0.2-mile "mining" tunnel that diverts most of the Etowah through a ridge, cutting off a 1-mile loop of the river. Below the mining tunnel, the river's pace slows as it enters the upper reaches of the valley known as Big Savannah, where the ruins of former hamlets haunt the riverbanks.

Outfitters Appalachian Outfitters (Dahlonega) is the nearest canoe and kayak outfitter.

## Points of Interest

MILE 23.2 (34.472192, -84.037442) Guy Rivers Cave & Shoal. Just below Castleberry Bridge is the "cave" of the gold robber Guy Rivers. Local legend holds that Guy earned his keep by stealing gold during the heyday of the region's gold rush. High on the bluff here is an overhanging rock that forms a cave-like structure. This, it is said, is where Guy hid his ill-gotten loot. The legend of Guy Rivers persisted for years, but historians now agree that the tale is fictional.

MILE 23.7 (34.471219, -84.039764) Shoal.

MILE 23.8 (34.469342, -84.037042) Shoal.

MILE 24.4 (34.465872, -84.036658) Shoal.

MILE 24.6 (34.467408, -84.038933) Shoal.

MILE 25.4 (34.460453, -84.044161) Gold Mining. The Weekend Gold Miners Club owns 136 acres on river left here. Prospectors have mined this land since the gold rush of 1828; today hobbyists still try their luck. The club has some 600 members who pay monthly membership fees for the right to use the property. It is not uncommon to see club members in the river using a dredge to sift through the sediment on the river bottom.

MILE 25.7 (34.454358, -84.045642) Shoal.

MILE 26.3 (34.450331, -84.048775) Shoal & Island.

MILE 26.6 (34.448325, -84.049467) Mining Tunnel. On river left here lies what is perhaps the most-talked-about feature on the Etowah—a cut that channels the bulk of the Etowah's flow through a 0.2-mile tunnel. The flow reenters the main channel of the river 1 mile downstream. The tunnel was begun in the 1890s in an effort to drain the Etowah to mine gold in the main channel that loops around this ridge, but it wasn't completed until 1932, when dynamite and jackhammers were used to finish the task. The gold deposits that were the expected reward of this ambitious endeavor never materialized. Today, a ride through the tunnel is a much-sought-after novelty, but one that should be undertaken with great care and only in medium to low flows. It should not be attempted if the proverbial "light at the end of the tunnel" cannot be seen or is obstructed. A small ledge in the middle of the tunnel provides added excitement. Local outfitters advise against it, saying "an entire outfitter store could be stocked with the gear lying at the bottom of that tunnel."

MILE 26.7 (34.448864, -84.050589) Shoal. An island that blocks the river just below the entrance to the tunnel marks the beginning of the alternative to the mining tunnel route. It is followed by a series of small shoals. Since much of the river's flow is diverted here, these shallow shoals can be particularly nettlesome.

MILE 27.1 (34.447844, -84.056156) Calhoun Creek & Reservoir. In 2011, a plan surfaced to build a water supply reservoir just upstream on this creek, bringing to three the number of proposed reservoirs within a 16-mile stretch of the Etowah in Dawson County. This proposal was unique in that its proponents were a private reservoir development company hoping to take advantage of a new law adopted by Georgia in 2011 facilitating private-public reservoir partnerships. Like the proposed Russell and Shoal Creek reservoirs downstream, this project

DOWNSTREAM OF CASTLEBERRY BRIDGE,
LUMPKIN COUNTY

would rely on water pumped from the Etowah River and it would also destroy habitat for the federally protected Cherokee darter. As proposed, the project would supply 47 million gallons a day (mgd) to Metro Atlanta. By contrast, studies by the Atlanta-based water protection group, Chattahoochee Riverkeeper, have shown that an aggressive program to replace toilets with low-flow models could save as much as 50 mgd in Metro Atlanta.

MILE 27.5 (34.445772, -84.051317) Tunnel Outlet. If you choose to run the Mining Tunnel, you emerge here.

MILE 28.3 (34.440597, -84.042408) Powerlines.

MILE 30.1 (34.423917, -84.023667) Dog Hobble. On river right here is a good place to see dog hobble, a plant common to stream banks in the southern Appalachians. Like its close relatives rhododendron and mountain laurel, this member of the heath family is an evergreen, making it easy to identify during the winter months. In the early spring it produces clusters of small, white bell-shaped blossoms. Its common name is derived from its dense tangle of arching branches that make traveling through it a chore. Hunters say that bears run through stands of dog hobble to distance themselves from pursuing hounds. The leaves and flower nectar are highly poisonous to both humans and animals.

DOWNSTREAM OF CASTLEBERRY BRIDGE,
DAWSON COUNTY

MILE 30.8 (34.414606, -84.019622) Landrum/Bamboo. The wooden structure on river right is the remains of Jenkins Mill and the community of Landrum. Landrum is one of four settlements that formed along the banks of the Etowah in Dawson County's "Big Savannah" valley during the 1800s. The mill, which was built between 1854 and 1866, harnessed the river's power to grind corn. Rock bridge piers just downstream mark the original crossing of the river in Landrum. Like the mill, the bamboo stand next to it is another imprint of humans on the landscape. Bamboo is a nonnative species, and the Georgia Exotic Pest Plant Council includes it on its list of threats to Georgia's natural areas. Bamboo quickly takes over the habitat of native species and can significantly alter ecosystems. It should not be confused with native river cane, a smaller cousin of the invasive bamboo. Zoo Atlanta, however, is making good use of Georgia's invasive bamboo; the zoo harvests bamboo from landowners who wish to contribute to feeding the zoo's pair of giant panda bears, who eat 220 pounds of the stuff each day.

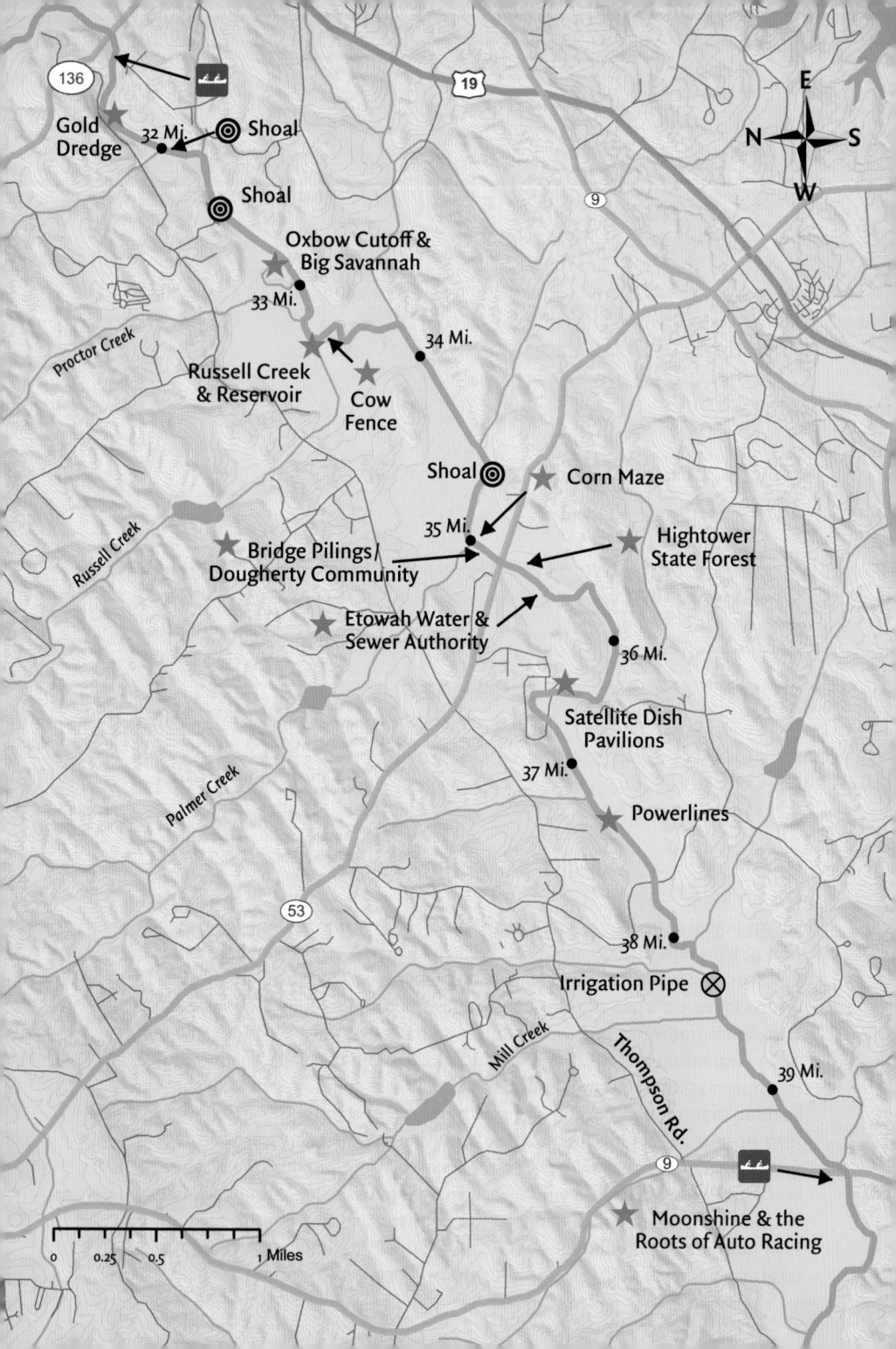

136

19

9

Gold
Dredge

32 Mi. ◎ Shoal

◎ Shoal

Oxbow Cutoff &
Big Savannah

33 Mi.

34 Mi.

Proctor Creek

Russell Creek
& Reservoir

Cow
Fence

Russell Creek

Shoal ◎

Corn Maze

35 Mi.

Bridge Pilings/
Dougherty Community

Hightower
State Forest

Etowah Water &
Sewer Authority

36 Mi.

Palmer Creek

Satellite Dish
Pavilions

37 Mi.

Powerlines

53

38 Mi.

Irrigation Pipe ⊗

39 Mi.

Mill Creek

Thompson Rd.

9

Moonshine & the
Roots of Auto Racing

E

N      S

W

0    0.25    0.5    1 Miles

# Big Savannah

**Length** 8.5 miles (Ga. 136 to Ga. 9)

**Class** 1

**Time** 3–6 hours

**Minimum Level** This section of river can be run except in the most severe droughts. Levels of 60 cubic feet per second or greater at the Hwy. 136 gauge should provide sufficient flow.

**River Gauge** The nearest river gauge is located at Ga. 136: http://waterdata.usgs.gov/ga /nwis/uv?site_no=02388975.

**Launch Site** There is no developed boat launch at this site. A pull-off on the north side of the highway just west of the river provides limited parking. The launch site is below the bridge and requires a carry of about 0.1 mile from the parking area. However, a sandbar provides an easy launch.

RIVER VIEW, DAWSON COUNTY

**DIRECTIONS** The launch is located on Ga. 136 north of Dawsonville. From the intersection of Ga. 400 and Ga. 136 north of Dawsonville, go west on Ga. 136 and proceed 0.9 mile to the Etowah River. The pull-off is on the right after the bridge.

**Take Out Site** The take out is located on river right just downstream of the Hwy. 9 bridge. This Dawson County facility includes a canoe and kayak launch, ample parking, and a portable toilet. Other amenities include a covered pavilion, informational kiosk, and benches and swings overlooking the river.

**DIRECTIONS** From the Hwy. 136 launch site, proceed west on Ga. 136 0.1 mile to Etowah River Road on left. Turn left and proceed 4 miles to Ga. 53. Continue across

Ga. 53 on Thompson Road an additional 2.5 miles. Turn left onto Ga. 9 and proceed 0.7 mile to the take out site on the right, just before the road crosses the bridge.

**Descriptions** Owing to its rich bottomlands, the Etowah's Big Savannah was among the first areas of Dawson County that was settled. As a result, as the Etowah winds through this valley, it is flanked by history at seemingly every turn. The shoals common upstream give way to slower moving water, and the scenery shifts from forest to field. For all its peaceful scenery, the valley may be best known as one of the birthplaces of stock car racing.

**Outfitters** Appalachian Outfitters (Dahlonega) is the nearest canoe and kayak outfitter.

## Points of Interest

**MILE 31.4 (34.409022, -84.024036) Gold Dredge.** Imagine a 90-foot-long, 25-foot-wide boat on the river here. Hard to imagine, but sitting on the river bottom near here are the remains of a wooden dredge barge that operated in this section of river from the 1890s through the 1920s. Speculators deployed the barge to dig sand and gravel from the river bottom in hopes of extracting gold. To move the barge upriver, they employed wenches tied to riverside trees. Powered by a steam engine, the wenches would haul the behemoth upriver and the shovels of the dredge would deepen the river as it went. The barge met its demise after one riverfront property owner denied the barge operators use of his trees.

**MILE 32 (34.405314, -84.029508) Shoal.**

**MILE 32.5 (34.401578, -84.034428) Shoal.**

**MILE 32.8 (34.396931, -84.038886) Oxbow Cutoff & Big Savannah.** On river right is a feature unusual to North Georgia rivers—an oxbow lake similar to those so common to the Coastal Plain rivers of South Georgia. Though not visible from water level, the pasture beyond the bank holds the shallow lake that was cut off as the Etowah carved a straighter course through this Dawson County valley known as Big Savannah. Some 2.5 miles long and nearly 1 mile wide, the Savannah is perhaps the most distinctive bottomlands in the county.

**MILE 33.4 (34.394944, -84.045417) Russell Creek & Reservoir.** Located just upstream on Russell Creek at river right is Head Lake, an 11-acre flood control reservoir built by the federal government in 1963. Hundreds of similar structures are scattered across Georgia, a legacy of an era when the feds aided farmers by keeping their bottomland fields from flooding. Now these aging structures are being eyed as water supply reservoirs for the region's growing population. Such is the case with Head Lake. The Etowah Water & Sewer Authority (EWSA) plans to expand the reservoir to 137 acres and pump water from the Etowah to fill it during periods of high flows in order to produce 17 million gallons of drinking water a day for Dawson County residents. Water is released from the dam to supplement flows on the Etowah as needed for withdrawals just downstream at the EWSA water intake facility. Improvements and expansions of existing reservoirs usually have fewer environmental impacts than new reservoirs, and the projects have the added benefit of rehabilitating these old, and sometimes unsafe, dams.

MILE 33.4 (34.394914, -84.045386) Cow Fence. A unique tire fence across the mouth of this creek on river right keeps cattle out of the river. Unfortunately, the cattle appear to have free rein within the tributary. When livestock congregate around streams, they contribute to bank erosion and—when they defecate— elevated bacteria levels. It should come as little surprise that in 2010 Georgia's Environmental Protection Division identified the next 8 miles of the Etowah as "polluted" due to high bacteria levels.

MILE 34.6 (34.382525, -84.056214) Shoal.

MILE 35 (34.384136, -84.061475) Corn Maze. On river left is Uncle Shuck's Corn Maze, a local attraction established in 2002. The maze boasts 12 acres of corn with some 4 miles of winding paths. It can take anywhere from 30 minutes to 2 hours to complete the challenge. Humankind has built mazes and labyrinths for centuries—most notably during the European Renaissance, when puzzle hedges were designed in estate gardens to amuse the aristocracy. Since the 1980s this art form has experienced a second renaissance. Since the first corn maze in the United States was cut in 1993, its popularity has grown at an amazing rate. In 2008, www.cornmazesamerica.com estimated that there were more than 800 in the United States. The brains behind the first U.S. corn maze was Don Frantz, a Broadway producer with Disney's *The Lion King* and *Beauty and the Beast* among his credits. He came upon the idea while flying cross-country. Staring down at the miles of corn fields, it dawned on him that it was possible to construct a maze without having to wait years to grow the hedgerows. In 1993, his first attempt was visited by 10,000 people and raised more than $55,000 for farmers victimized by flooding.

MILE 35.1 (34.383600, -84.061925) Bridge Pilings / Dougherty Community. The stone pilings here mark the site of a former bridge that crossed the Etowah into Dougherty, one of several circa 1800s towns that grew up in this fertile valley. The community centerpiece was a gristmill at the mouth of Palmer Creek on river right. The mill operated until the 1930s.

MILE 35.4 (34.380119, -84.064033) Hightower State Forest. On river left below the Ga. 53 bridge is the Georgia Forestry Commission's 142-acre Hightower Forest. The site was originally used as a nursery and seed orchard by the commission. Today it houses the Dawson County Fire Control unit.

MILE 35.5 (34.379339, -84.064850) Etowah Water & Sewer Authority. On river right is the raw water intake structure for the Etowah Water & Sewer Authority. After it designed its intake structure to better protect federally threatened and endangered Etowah and amber darters that live in this run of the river, EWSA is now permitted to withdraw up to 5.5 million gallons a day. The intake is built to withdraw water from a broader area to reduce the force of the suction and includes a fine screen that further prevents the fish from being pumped into the pipes—a common problem with intakes that pump large amounts of water. Just downstream from the intake is a wastewater discharge, which is active when filters at the water-treatment plant are backwashed.

MILE 36.3 (34.377147, -84.074342) Satellite Dish Pavilions. What's to be done with all those obsolete satellite dishes that litter backyards across North Georgia? Riverside landowners here have found a use—flip them over, attach long legs, and use them as pavilions.

MILE 37.4 (34.374322, -84.084583) Powerlines.

MILE 38.5 (34.366928, -84.098150) Irrigation Pipe. Riverfront landowners can pump up to 100,000 gallons a day from the Etowah without obtaining a permit from Georgia's Environmental Protection Division. Georgia operates under a regulated riparian rights law, meaning that landowners have the right to the reasonable use of water flowing by their land, but that right must be balanced with the rights of other users. Thus, the state regulates water withdrawals to protect the rights of all landowners.

MILE 39.6 (34.357536, -84.113581) Moonshine & the Roots of Auto Racing. Somewhere in the bottomlands of Big Savannah during the 1930s, Dawson County's fastest moonshine runners would gather on Sunday afternoon for races, placing bets on who had the fastest cars. Among the men at these gatherings were Raymond Parks, Lloyd Seay, and Roy Hall. The trio became legends in stock car racing. Parks, the car owner for both Seay and Hall, was a founder of NASCAR racing, and his car won the first NASCAR championship in 1949. Hall dominated the racing circuit in the late 1930s and 1940s and was a multiple winner at the Daytona track. Seay won numerous races driving Parks's cars from 1938 to 1941. All three men did time in prison—Parks and Seay for running moonshine, Hall for spinning "donuts" on Main Street in Daytona Beach. After his arrest and night in jail, Hall claimed he planned the incident, saying, "the motel rates are too high in this town." Seay's career was cut short in 1941 when he was shot and killed by a family member in a dispute over debt involving moonshine. Of course, Dawson County's racing history didn't end there—the county's most famous native son and resident is Bill Elliott, a winner of 44 NASCAR races who has amassed some $73 million in race winnings since 1976. The area's racing history is immortalized at the Georgia Racing Hall of Fame in nearby Dawsonville, and it all started in these bottomlands.

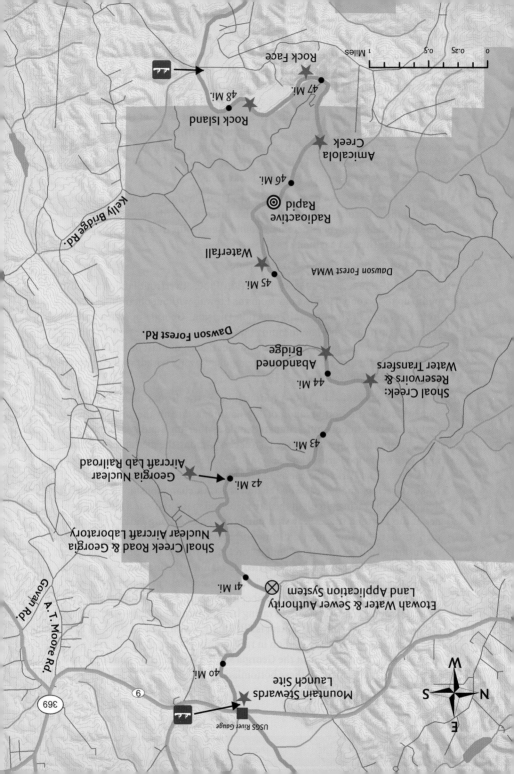

Rock Face

Rock Island

47 Mi.

48 Mi.

Amicalola
Creek

46 Mi.

Radioactive Rapid

Waterfall

Dawson Forest WMA

45 Mi.

Dawson Forest Rd.

Abandoned
Bridge

Shoal Creek:
Reservoirs &
Water Transfers

44 Mi.

43 Mi.

Georgia Nuclear
Aircraft Lab Railroad

42 Mi.

Shoal Creek Road & Georgia
Nuclear Aircraft Laboratory

Etowah Water & Sewer Authority
Land Application System

41 Mi.

Kelly Bridge Rd.

Govan Rd.

A. T. Moore Rd.

369

9

40 Mi.

USGS River Gauge

Mountain Stewards
Launch Site

0     0.25     0.5     1 Miles

N  W  E  S

# Dawson Forest

**Length** 9 miles (Ga. 9 to Kelly Bridge Road)

**Class** 1

**Time** 4–7 hours

**Minimum Level** This section of river can be run except during the most severe droughts. Levels of 60 cubic feet per second or greater at the Hwy. 9 gauge should provide sufficient flow.

---

**River Gauge** The nearest river gauge is located at Ga. 9: http://waterdata.usgs.gov /ga/nwis/uv?site_no=02389150.

**Launch Site** This Dawson County facility includes a canoe and kayak launch, ample parking, and a portable toilet. Other amenities include a covered pavilion, informational kiosk, and benches and swings overlooking the river.

DIRECTIONS The launch is located on Ga. 9 south of Dawsonville. From the intersection of Ga. 400 and Ga. 369 north of Cumming, turn left on Ga. 369 (Browns Bridge Road) and proceed 1 mile. Turn right onto Ga. 9 and proceed 7.8 miles to the Etowah River. The launch area is on your left after the bridge.

**Take Out Site** The take out is located on river right just before reaching Kelly Bridge. At this privately owned boat ramp, there is a nominal fee for the privilege of using the site (paid on the honor system at a drop box located on the gate into the parking area). The site features a paved boat ramp, ample parking, and a portable toilet.

DIRECTIONS From the Hwy. 9 launch site, turn right onto Ga. 9 and proceed 1.6 miles to A. T. Moore Road on the right. Turn right and proceed 0.7 mile to where A. T. Moore merges with Govan Road to become Kelly Bridge Road. Proceed from here 5.5 miles to the Etowah River. The take out is on your right after the bridge.

**Descriptions** Encompassing perhaps the most frequently paddled section on the entire length of the river, this 9-mile trip winds almost entirely within the beautiful 10,000-acre Dawson Forest Wildlife Management Area. The river here is intimate and shaded with several shoals. Though a wilderness feel emanates from the river's banks, the area was once teaming with people. From 1956 to 1971, government contractors worked on a top-secret project to build a nuclear-powered airplane. Today it is a haven for paddlers, hikers, bikers, hunters, anglers, and horseback riders. The primary obstacles to navigation are the cross-river strainers that occur frequently. All shoals are rated as Class 1 in difficulty.

**Outfitters** Appalachian Outfitters (Dahlonega) is the nearest canoe and kayak outfitter.

## Points of Interest

MILE 39.5 (34.357514, -84.114064) Mountain Stewards Launch Site. Built in 2009, this Dawson County–maintained launch site is another feather in the cap of a community that promotes itself as an outdoor recreation magnet. Like many of the launches along the Etowah, its development was a cooperative effort between a local government, a private landowner, and a nonprofit organization, in this case the Mountain Stewards, which restores and builds recreational trails in North Georgia. This group has designed and constructed numerous boat launches, opening 34 miles of canoe routes in North Georgia between 2005 and 2010

MILE 40.7 (34.361294, -84.131064) Etowah Water & Sewer Authority Land Application System. On river right is the EWSA wastewater treatment facility, which treats about a half million gallons of sewage through a land application system. After sewage is initially treated, the effluent is sprayed on the land surrounding the facility. The advantage of this system is that wastewater is not discharged directly to the river. The disadvantage is that less water is returned immediately to the river—an increasing concern as more and more people depend upon the river for drinking water. EWSA's future plans call for the development of a new facility that can treat up to 10 million gallons a day and return treated water directly to the river.

MILE 41.6 (34.356094, -84.139814) Shoal Creek Road & Georgia Nuclear Aircraft Laboratory. This spot marks the river's entry into the Dawson Forest Wildlife Management Area, a 10,000-acre tract that flanks the river on both sides for the next 5 miles. You would hardly guess it from the looks of things today, but from 1956 until 1971, engineers with Lockheed Aircraft Corp. tried to build a nuclear-powered airplane at this site for the U.S. Air Force. In the process, they also conducted rather frightening tests on the effects of radiation. Signs remain of the Georgia Nuclear Aircraft Laboratory (GNAL), including the water intake structure just downstream of the bridge here. Abandoned bridge piers at several sites on the river mark the locations of roads and a railroad system that linked the lab's facilities, which included a nuclear reactor, a cooling site, and a hot-cell building. The compound even contained an underground shielded site, where employees sheltered when the reactor was operational, and an underground parking facility.

Although the plane was a bust, other radioactive-material-related research was performed at GNAL. In these tests a 10-megawatt radiation effects reactor was used to expose various materials to radiation to study the effects. This reactor was housed in a large metal building that offered no protection for the surrounding area. In fact, low levels of radiation can still be found in 3 acres of the

forest, which remain restricted. When not in use, the reactor was submerged in a swimming pool–like structure filled with water from the Etowah. The land is now owned by the City of Atlanta, which purchased it with intentions of building a second airport. The Georgia Forestry Commission has managed the forest, which includes 27 miles of hiking, biking, and equestrian trails, since 1975.

MILE 41.9 (34.356253, -84.146744) Georgia Nuclear Aircraft Lab Railroad.

MILE 43.6 (34.373028, -84.160925) Shoal Creek: Reservoirs & Water Transfers. On river right here, Shoal Creek spills into the Etowah. Shoal Creek has been called the epicenter of the biodiversity in the Upper Etowah River basin because of its healthy fish populations, including the federally protected Etowah and Cherokee darters. About 0.2 mile upstream is the proposed site of a dam that will inundate 1,200 acres of the forest for a water supply reservoir. The project, which has been under consideration since the early 1990s, would create a pool designed to meet regional water needs, including those of Metro Atlanta. Water would be pumped from the Etowah to fill the reservoir and then piped 40 miles to Metro Atlanta through a process known as an interbasin transfer. Such transfers involve moving water from one river basin to another without returning that water to the river of origin. Water transfers have become one of the most controversial water management practices in Georgia because they deprive downstream communities of the use of the water and can threaten healthy flows. One scenario presented for the Shoal Creek Reservoir would send 100 million gallons a day to Metro Atlanta, an amount almost equal to the water flowing down the river during annual low-flow periods. A dam on Shoal Creek would eliminate some of the last high-quality habitat for protected fish in the Etowah River basin.

MILE 44.2 (34.368342, -84.164997) Abandoned Bridge.

MILE 45.2 (34.361258, -84.178181) Waterfall. A short walk up the small tributary on river left here leads you to a beautiful waterfall.

MILE 45.7 (34.361975, -84.186789) Radioactive Rapid. The one shoal of significance on this section of river is marked by an island that splits the current. During low water, the preferred route is on far river left, where you descend over a pair of short shelves. High water makes a path around either side of the island possible. Those not wishing to paddle the rapid can portage, beginning at the head of the island.

MILE 46.6 (34.367639, -84.196347) Amicalola Creek. Sometimes referred to as the Amicalola River, this stream has its beginnings above Amicalola Falls. At 729 feet, Amicalola Falls is the tallest cascading waterfall east of the Mississippi. The river itself is a whitewater destination, best known for the aptly named Edge of the World rapid. *Amicalola* is a Cherokee word that means "tumbling waters."

MILE 47.2 (34.366036, -84.204783) Rock Face. The impressive rock bluff on river right provides a glimpse of the region's geologic history. On its course from the mountains to Rome, the river cuts through three distinct geological areas—Eastern Blue Ridge, Western Blue Ridge, and Ridge and Valley. The Eastern Blue Ridge represents an intraoceanic volcanic arc (similar to the present-day Philippines) that is 500–550 million years old. The Western Blue Ridge comprises North American sedimentary rocks that were deeply buried and metamorphosed during accretion of the Eastern Blue Ridge and formation of the Appalachian Mountain system. The Ridge and Valley is underlain by North American sedimentary rocks that were folded during Appalachian mountain building.

MILE 47.7 (34.359064, -84.200714) Rock Island. A rock island splits the river here and creates a fun shoal between river left and the island. The massive eddy and pool on the downstream side of the rock form an excellent swimming hole.

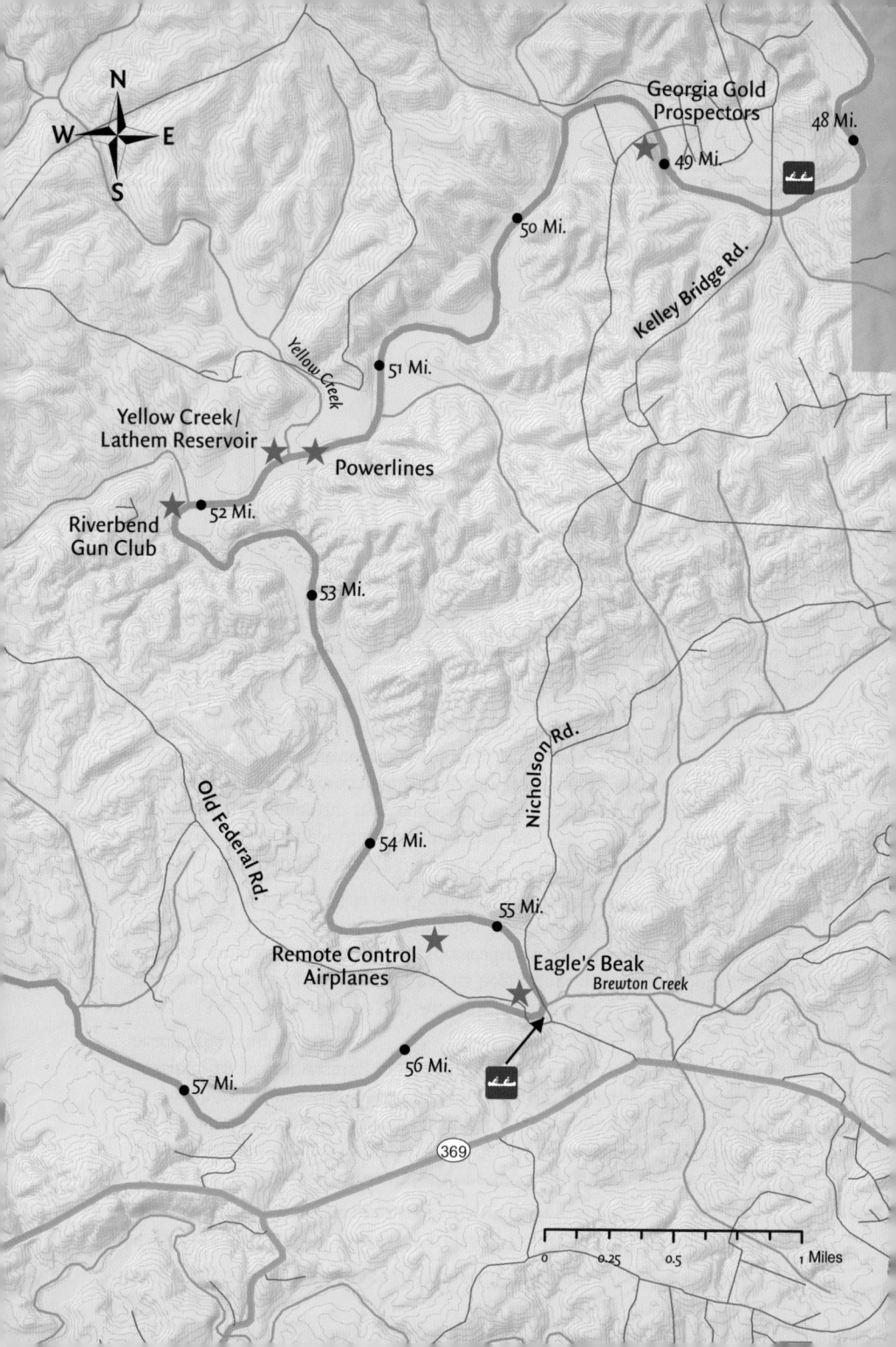

# Eagle's Beak

Length  7 miles (Kelly Bridge Road to Old Federal Road)

Class  1

Time  3–5 hours

Minimum Level  This section of river is runnable except in the most severe droughts. Anything above 60 cubic feet per second at the Hwy. 9 gauge should provide sufficient flow.

---

River Gauge  The nearest upstream river gauge is located at Ga. 9 near Dawsonville: http://waterdata.usgs.gov/ga/nwis/uv?site_no=02389150.

Launch Site  At this privately owned boat ramp, there is a nominal fee for the privilege of using the site (paid on the honor system at a drop box located on the gate into the parking area). The site includes a paved boat ramp, ample parking, and a portable toilet.

DIRECTIONS  The launch is located on Kelly Bridge Road, west of Ga. 9. From the intersection of Ga. 400 and Ga. 369 north of Cumming, turn left onto Ga. 369 (Browns Bridge Road) and proceed 1 mile. Turn right onto Ga. 9 and proceed 6.2 miles. Turn left onto A. T. Moore Road and proceed 0.7 mile to where A. T. Moore

EAGLE'S BEAK VIEW, DAWSON COUNTY

merges with Govan Road to become Kelly Bridge Road. Proceed from here 5.5 miles to the Etowah River. The launch area is on your right after Kelly Bridge.

Take Out Site The take out is located on river left just before you reach the Old Federal Road Bridge. It is possible to take out beneath the bridge, although strainers pinned against the bridge piers often make this difficult. The take out is up steep banks. There is no developed launch or parking area at this location.

DIRECTIONS From the Kelly Bridge Road launch site, turn left on Kelly Bridge Road and proceed 2.2 miles. Turn right onto Needham Road and proceed 0.4 mile. Turn right onto Nicholson Road and proceed 3.3 miles to Old Federal Road; the take out site is on the right before reaching Old Federal Road.

Descriptions Though the river leaves behind the protected corridor formed by the Dawson Forest Wildlife Management Area, the 7 miles from Kelly Bridge remains rural and the riverbanks undeveloped. Perhaps for that reason it and the land surrounding it are the play places for some unique recreational groups, including a gold mining association, a gun club, and a remote-control airplane club. The river runs calm with no significant shoals or rapids, though occasionally strainers can block all, or a portion, of the river.

Outfitters Appalachian Outfitters (Dahlonega) is the nearest canoe and kayak outfitter.

## Points of Interest

MILE 49.1 (34.356125, -84.213728) Georgia Gold Prospectors. Just below Kelly Bridge is land owned by Georgia Gold Prospectors Association. The group of 250 recreational prospectors holds regular outings on numerous claims in Georgia. One of the common techniques for finding gold in the river is to deploy a small floating dredge. The dredge sucks sand and gravel from the river bottom and sends it through a sluice constructed with horizontal ridges or bars that catch the heaviest particles in the slurry. Gold, being very dense, stays in the sluice box because of its weight. Usually, the contents of the sluice are then transferred to a gold pan, where the fine particles of gold can be collected by hand.

GOLD MINING DREDGE, DAWSON COUNTY

MILE 51.4 (34.339267, -84.236956) Powerlines.

MILE 51.5 (34.338706, -84.239347) Yellow Creek / Lathem Reservoir. About 2 miles upstream on Yellow Creek sits the Cherokee County Water & Sewerage Authority's (CCWSA) 411-acre Hollis Lathem Reservoir. The project, considered a drought contingency reservoir, was built when the CCWSA needed to increase its water withdrawal downstream on the Etowah in the early 1990s. Water from the reservoir is released downstream when the Etowah dips below a certain level, allowing the CCWSA to keep water flowing to homes and businesses in Cherokee County.

It is one of two water supply reservoirs built since 1990 to serve Cherokee County residents. Increased water demands and the proliferation of water supply projects like Lathem are among the biggest threats to the health and biodiversity of the Etowah. Lathem, and Hickory Log Reservoir downstream, both destroyed critical habitat for the federally protected Cherokee darter, a fish found in the Etowah River basin and nowhere else in the world.

MILE 52.1 (34.336172, -84.245508) Riverbend Gun Club. This private shooting range caters to some 1,600 gun enthusiasts who pay annual membership dues to use the club's ten firing ranges. Originally located on the Chattahoochee River in North Fulton County, the club is part of the story of Atlanta's sprawl since the 1980s. In Fulton County, upscale neighbors pushed their noisy neighbors north to Forsyth County. As that county grew, the club sought more secluded surroundings, landing here in Dawson County. As you paddle past this facility, you might well hear gun shots coming from the club's controlled ranges.

MILE 54.7 (34.313642, -84.228511) Remote Control Airplanes. First guns, now planes! On river right here is the home of the Georgia Model Aviators, a private club that maintains 66 acres along the river as an airfield for remote-control flying machines. You can often hear planes flying over the river and might also see them.

MILE 55.4 (34.309694, -84.221553) Eagle's Beak. So called because the route the Etowah takes here resembles a bird's beak and body. At this location, you are on the top of the beak, and the stretch that runs parallel to Old Federal Road below the take out forms the bottom of the beak. The tip of the beak is the river's sharp bend at Old Federal Road. Forsyth County owns the property on river right below the bridge and has plans to develop the land as a public park. The park is to include canoe and kayak launches on the river.

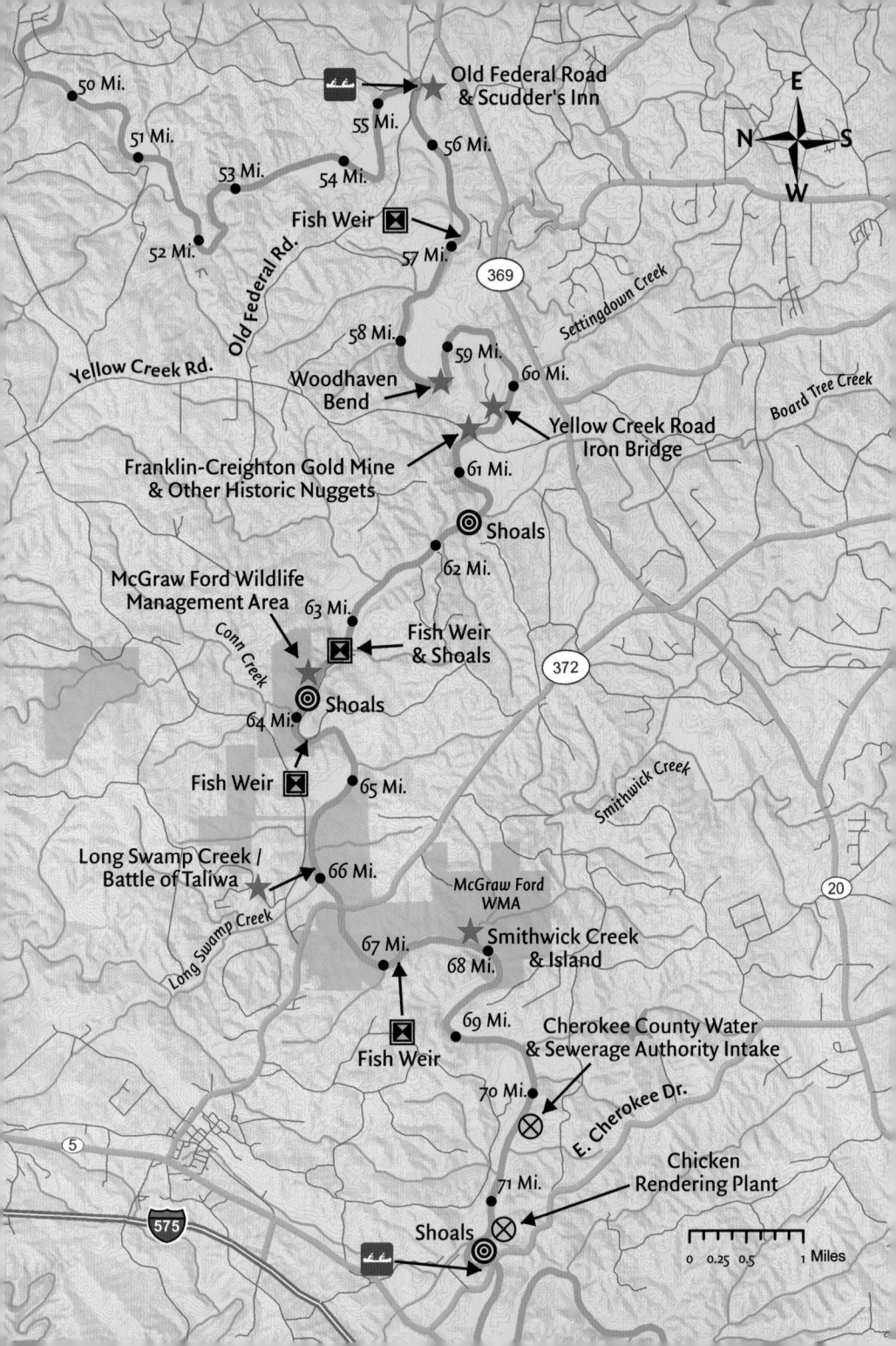

50 Mi.

51 Mi.

53 Mi.

54 Mi.

52 Mi.

55 Mi.

56 Mi.

Old Federal Road
& Scudder's Inn

Fish Weir

57 Mi.

369

Settingdown Creek

Board Tree Creek

Old Federal Rd.

Yellow Creek Rd.

58 Mi.

59 Mi.

60 Mi.

Woodhaven
Bend

Yellow Creek Road
Iron Bridge

Franklin-Creighton Gold Mine
& Other Historic Nuggets

61 Mi.

Shoals

62 Mi.

McGraw Ford Wildlife
Management Area

63 Mi.

Conn Creek

Fish Weir
& Shoals

372

Shoals

64 Mi.

Fish Weir

65 Mi.

Smithwick Creek

Long Swamp Creek /
Battle of Taliwa

66 Mi.

McGraw Ford
WMA

Smithwick Creek
& Island

20

Long Swamp Creek

67 Mi.

68 Mi.

Fish Weir

69 Mi.

Cherokee County Water
& Sewerage Authority Intake

70 Mi.

E. Cherokee Dr.

Chicken
Rendering Plant

5

71 Mi.

Shoals

575

0   0.25  0.5        1 Miles

N   E
W   S

# McGraw Ford

Length 16 miles (Old Federal Road to East Cherokee Drive)

Class 1

Time 7–10 hours

Minimum Level Numerous shoals within the McGraw Ford Wildlife Management Area make this run difficult at levels below 130 cubic feet per second at the Ga. 9 gauge near Dawsonville. If you run it below these levels, be prepared to do some walking.

---

River Gauge The nearest upstream river gauge is located at Ga. 9 near Dawsonville: http://waterdata.usgs.gov/ga/nwis/uv?site_no=02389150.

Launch Site There is no developed launch site at Old Federal Road, although Forsyth County is developing the property surrounding Old Federal Road as Eagle's Beak Park. The plans include boat launches. Access is on the east side of the river at the corner of Nicholson Road and Old Federal Road. The launch site is extremely steep, but boats can be slid down the embankment or carried beneath the bridge to gain river access.

DIRECTIONS The launch is located off Old Federal Road, west of Ga. 369. From the intersection of Ga. 400 and Ga. 369 north of Cumming, go west on Ga. 369 (Browns Bridge Road) and proceed 8.5 miles. Turn right onto Old Federal Road and proceed 0.3 mile. Turn right onto Nicholson Road. The launch area is on your left.

Take Out Site The take out is located on river right opposite the chicken rendering plant, within sight of the East Cherokee Road bridge. A sandbar provides for an easy take out. There is no developed launch or parking area.

DIRECTIONS From the intersection of Old Federal Road and Ga. 369, turn right (west) onto Ga. 369 and proceed 7.5 miles to Ga. 20. Turn right onto Ga. 20 and proceed 2 miles to East Cherokee Drive. Turn right onto East Cherokee Drive and proceed 6.4 miles to the Etowah River. Cross the bridge. Access to the take out is on the right.

Descriptions This section is highlighted by the beautiful shoals in the McGraw Ford Wildlife Management Area that harbor much of the Etowah's fish diversity, including the federally protected Etowah darter. Along the way it flows over fish weirs, past significant Native American and gold mining sites, and even lends its water to North Georgia's chicken industry at the chicken rendering plant. The shoals of McGraw Ford are the primary obstacle to navigation, though the stretch between

Old Federal Road and Settingdown Creek is frequently clogged with cross-river strainers that require portages.

Outfitters Lilydipper Outfitters in Canton is the nearest canoe and kayak outfitter.

## Points of Interest

MILE 55.5 (34.308528, -84.221361) Old Federal Road & Scudder's Inn. You would hardly suspect it now, but this two-lane road was once the major thoroughfare by which early settlers entered the Cherokee Nation of North Georgia. A trading path as early as 1731, the old route evolved into the Federal Road through the efforts of private enterprise rather than the federal government. Among the most important were the Cherokees, who constructed portions of the road in exchange for the right to operate inns and stores as well as ferries on the more than 80 streams and rivers that the road traversed. In the 1820s, the going rate for a ferry crossing was $1 for a wagon and four horses, 50¢ for a man and horse, and 1¢ each for hogs, sheep, and goats. It remains unclear whether a ferry operated at this crossing of the Etowah. Enterprising whites also moved in to profit off travelers, often resulting in conflicts with the Cherokees. A quarter mile east of the river here, U.S. citizen Jacob Scudder operated an inn from 1817 to 1831 and refused to pay taxes to the Cherokees for that privilege. The Cherokees retaliated with fines and the seizure of some of his property. With the even-

SHOALS AT MCGRAW FORD, CHEROKEE COUNTY

tual removal of the Cherokees and the advent of new roads, use of the Federal Road declined. Railroads further reduced the road's significance. It is believed that Fort Campbell, a Cherokee removal site that operated from April to June 1838, sat along the banks of the Etowah here. It was here that local Cherokees were rounded up before their forced migration west to Oklahoma.

MILE 56.8 (34.302733, -84.244211) Fish Weir.

MILE 58.5 (34.304108, -84.264789) Woodhaven Bend. At this bend in the river are a boat launch and pavilion, marking the start of the upscale Woodhaven Bend subdivision that the Etowah winds around for the next 2 miles. The equestrian estate neighborhood was the vision of Robin Loudermilk, CEO of the Atlanta-based rent-to-own company, Aaron Rents. The upscale equestrian subdivision incorporates a 150-foot buffer along the river, giving all residents of the community access to the river via walking paths and several boat launches—a plan that better protects the river corridor and better serves the residents. In other developments along the Etowah, the riverfront is divided into lots, excluding other homeowners from river access.

MILE 60.4 (34.298531, -84.272108) Yellow Creek Road Iron Bridge. The remains of the iron bridge mark this former route of Yellow Creek Road and the site of a tragic incident in 1905 involving the superintendent of the Franklin-Creighton Gold Mine, which likely precipitated the construction of the bridge. This account appeared in the April 28, 1905, issue of the *Rome News-Tribune*: "A terrible tragedy was enacted at Creighton Wednesday afternoon when Edward Axson, wife and baby were drowned in the Etowah river. Mr. Axson accompanied by his wife and child were going to a picnic a few miles distant from Creighton. He was driving a nettlesome span of horses. About one-fourth of a mile from the river the horses ran away. Instead of a bridge the river is crossed by means of a flat and this is always left on the bank directly in the path of the road. The horses dashed across the flat, carrying their human burden and plunged into the river, which was about 15 feet deep at this place. Mr. Axson sought to rescue his wife and child. He gathered them under each arm and struggled to gain the task, but it was too great a burden. The bodies of Mrs. Axson and baby were washed towards the dam and were found immediately. Mr. Axson's body was not found until late yesterday." This was of particular interest to Romans as Axson was a native son, the brother of Ellen Axson Wilson, wife of Woodrow Wilson who in 1913 would become the country's 28th president. The remains of the dam mentioned in this news story lie just around the bend.

MILE 60.5 (34.299678, -84.272553) Franklin-Creighton Gold Mine & Other Historic Nuggets. The cross-river shoal at this location marks the site of a dam that helped power the Franklin-Creighton Gold Mine—the history of which tells a series of tragic stories. In the early 1830s, an English immigrant, John Pascoe, established a mine near this site that proved successful, but he became a victim of his own prosperity. He died of mercury poisoning in 1853, the result of constant exposure to mercury in the gold ore processing operation. Rumors of gold bars being buried with him led to so many robbers digging up his grave at nearby Hightower Baptist Church that his coffin was eventually removed and interned at an undisclosed location on his plantation. The legacy of mercury has lasted much longer than the gold did. Even today, fish caught from the Etowah River have been found to contain unhealthy levels of mercury

SHOALS AT MCGRAW FORD,
CHEROKEE COUNTY

and some of it is believed to be the result of mercury's extensive use at mining operations during the 1800s. The other notable miner at this site was Mary G. Franklin, a widow who drew a 40-acre lot in the 1932 land lottery. Shortly after acquiring the property, she had dozens of offers for her holding. With her curiosity piqued, Mrs. Franklin decided she should investigate her new property. When she arrived, she found a score of men shoveling dirt and panning gold. Mrs. Franklin had the men removed and began working the lot herself, along with her family. Her efforts ultimately led to the development of one of the area's most successful gold mines. In 1882, northern investors bought into her operation and expanded it. By 1896 the site held a complete mining plant with large stamp mill, chlorination plant, assay laboratory, blacksmith shop, stables, miners' cottages, and the Etowah River dam with two large turbines to generate power for the site. In 1913, a mine shaft collapsed beneath the river, filling the mines with water and making further operation of the plant financially infeasible.

MILE 61.8 (34.302125, -84.286717) Shoals. This is the first set of three shoals on this run of river. In low water, pick your route carefully to avoid walking. The shoals extend 0.2 mile.

MILE 63.4 (34.318961, -84.306222) Fish Weir & Shoals. This set of shoals ends with a distinct V-shaped fish weir on the right side of the river.

MILE 63.5 (34.321225, -84.309228) McGraw Ford Wildlife Management Area. A state wildlife management area (WMA) encompassing 2,400 acres, including some of the most picturesque paddling to be found on the Etowah, starts here on river right. The WMA extends 4 miles downstream to around Smithwick Creek and includes a patchwork of parcels on both sides of the river.

MILE 63.6 (34.321672, -84.310492) Shoals. This third and final set of shoals extends more than 0.2 mile to Conn Creek.

MILE 64.5 (34.320919, -84.318081) Fish Weir. This is perhaps one of the most distinctive weirs in Cherokee County. The V-shaped structures were built by the Native inhabitants 500–1,000 years ago. They worked simply. At the top of the V, a long line of people would wade downstream, spooking the fish to the point of the V. Other people would be waiting at the point with a basket to capture the frightened fish.

MILE 66 (34.320789, -84.339225) Long Swamp Creek / Battle of Taliwa. Around 1755, where Long Swamp and the Etowah meet, the Battle of Taliwa was fought. Some 500 Cherokees under the direction of Oconostota defeated a larger band of Creeks. Among the Cherokee warriors there was at least one heroine, Nancy Ward or Nan'yehi—the 18-year-old wife of the Cherokee known as Kingfisher. When Kingfisher was slain in the battle, Nan'yehi took up his gun and continued the fight. Reportedly, her courage led the Cherokee in a rout of the enemy. So complete was the defeat that the Creeks retreated permanently south of the Chattahoochee River, and Nan'yehi earned the title of honor: Beloved Woman. She later married Bryant Ward, a white man who took up residence among the Cherokees, and she adopted the name Nancy. She became an outspoken supporter of peace with white settlers. She died in 1822.

MILE 67.3 (34.310450, -84.350103) Fish Weir.

MILE 67.7 (34.302878, -84.348808) Smithwick Creek & Island.

MILE 70.4 (34.296075, -84.376275) Cherokee County Water & Sewerage Authority Intake. This large structure on river left is the intake facility for the Cherokee County Water & Sewerage Authority. CCWSA supplies about 14 million gallons a day (mgd) of water to 130,000 people. During periods of low flow, water releases from the CCWSA Hollis Lathem Reservoir on Yellow Creek upstream ensure adequate flows for continued withdrawals. Like many water providers in Georgia, the CCWSA saw a significant decline in water demand following the drought of 2007–2008. Prior to the drought, the CCWSA pumped as much as 25 mgd, but since then drought-related watering restrictions and water conservation measures have helped reduced peak demand by about 7 mgd. More efficient use of water is good news for the river, the critters that live in it, and downstream communities also dependent on the Etowah for their drinking water.

MILE 71.3 (34.301194, -84.393408) Chicken Rendering Plant. The facility on river left pumps about 14 million gallons of the Etowah each week to turn 7 million pounds of chicken parts—feet, heads, entrails, and such—into the makings of chicken feed and pet food. The facility's wastewater discharge is located downstream opposite the take out.

MILE 71.7 (34.300678, -84.396861) Shoal.

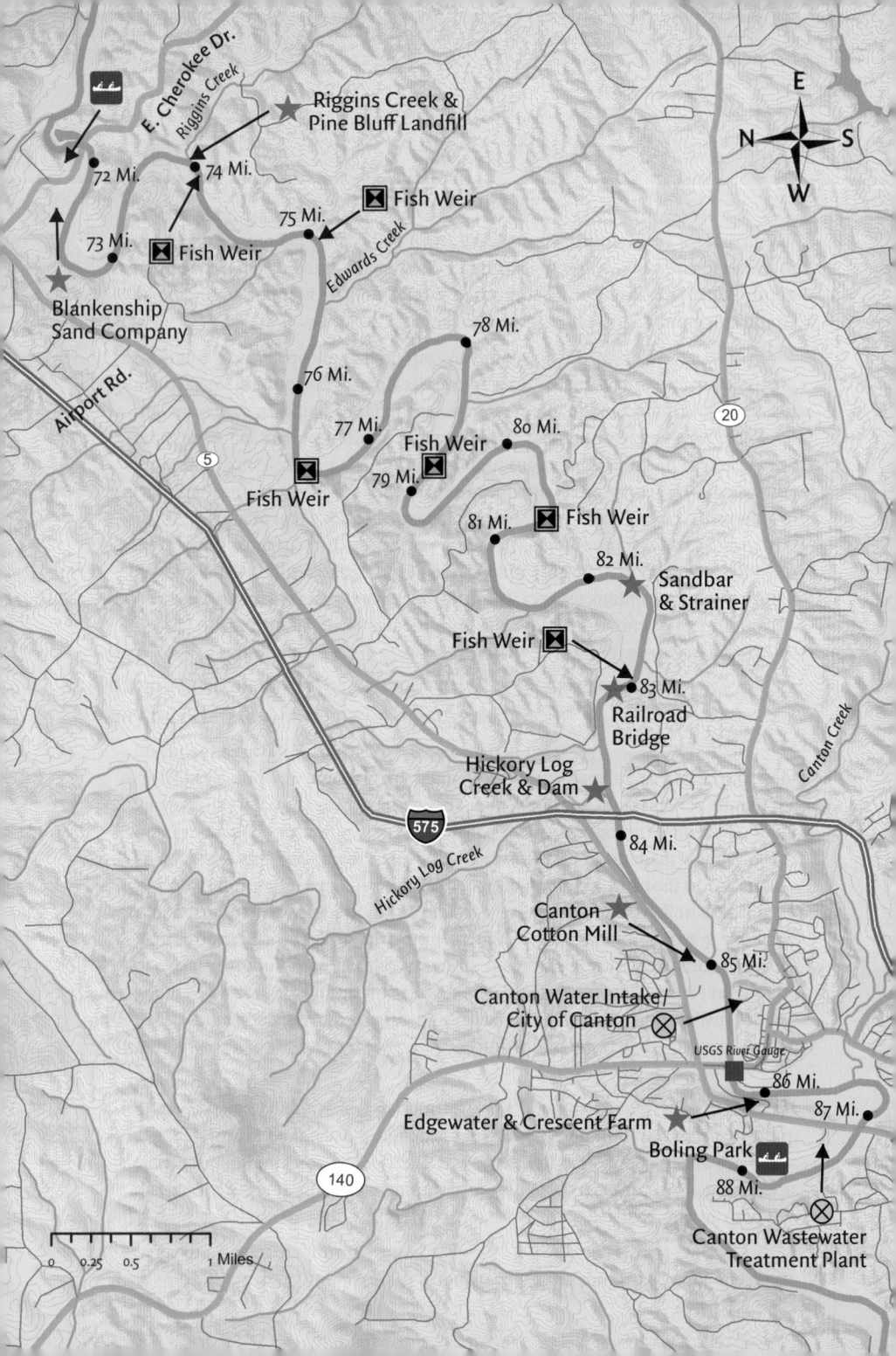

E. Cherokee Dr.

Riggins Creek

72 Mi.

74 Mi.

Riggins Creek &
Pine Bluff Landfill

75 Mi.

Fish Weir

73 Mi.

Fish Weir

Blankenship
Sand Company

Edwards Creek

Airport Rd.

76 Mi.

78 Mi.

5

77 Mi.

Fish Weir

79 Mi.

80 Mi.

Fish Weir

81 Mi.

Fish Weir

82 Mi.

Sandbar
& Strainer

Fish Weir

83 Mi.

Railroad
Bridge

Canton Creek

20

Hickory Log
Creek & Dam

575

84 Mi.

Hickory Log Creek

Canton
Cotton Mill

85 Mi.

Canton Water Intake/
City of Canton

USGS River Gauge

86 Mi.

Edgewater & Crescent Farm

87 Mi.

Boling Park

88 Mi.

140

Canton Wastewater
Treatment Plant

N E S W

0   0.25   0.5        1 Miles

# Canton

Length  16 miles (East Cherokee Drive to Boling Park)

Class  1

Time  7–10 hours

Minimum Level  This section of river is suitable for running at all times, although during severe drought some shoals may be difficult to navigate.

---

River Gauge  The nearest river gauge is located at Canton: http://waterdata.usgs.gov/ga/nwis/uv?site_no=02392000.

Launch Site  Access to the river is on the north side of the river opposite the chicken rendering plant at a location known locally as Gober Beach. There is no developed launch or parking area, but a gentle slope to the river and wide sandbar make for a suitable launch.

DIRECTIONS  The launch is located off Ga. 5 near Ball Ground. From Exit 24 on I-575 north of Canton, travel south on Airport Road for 0.5 mile. Turn left onto Ga. 5 and proceed 1 mile. Turn right onto East Cherokee Drive and proceed 0.8 mile to the river and the launch area on the left.

Take Out Site  The take out is located in the City of Canton's Boling Park on river right. There is not a developed boat launch at this location, but it is possible to take out from the river's steep bank adjacent to the picnic area located between the soccer fields and the tennis courts.

DIRECTIONS  From the launch site on East Cherokee Drive, return to Ga. 5. Turn left and proceed 1 mile. Turn right onto Airport Road and proceed 0.5 mile to I-575. Take I-575 south to Canton and proceed 7.2 miles to Exit 16 (Ga. 20 West). Take Ga. 20 west for 0.6 mile to the traffic light at Ga. 140 / Ga. 20. Turn right and proceed 0.4 mile. Turn left into Boling Park and proceed 0.4 mile to the picnic area on the left.

Outfitters  Lilydipper Outfitters in Canton is the nearest canoe and kayak outfitter.

Description  Though it passes through the heart of one of the country's fastest growing counties, the Etowah in Cherokee County remains surprisingly wild as it winds snakelike from East Cherokee Drive to Canton. Featuring six Native American fish weirs, this section of river, while a window to the past, runs headlong into 21st-century demands, including landfills, water supply reservoirs, and wastewater treatment plants. Though mostly flatwater, the river periodically quickens its pace over small shoals and fish weirs.

## Points of Interest

MILE 72.4 (34.300275, -84.403614) Blankenship Sand Company. The self-proclaimed "cleaners of the Etowah," the Blankenship Sand Company dredges sand and silt from the river bottom here and downstream on the upper end of Lake Allatoona. The barge you see sucks sand and water from the river and pumps it onto the shore, where it is separated for our use and enjoyment. The sand is used to make concrete, finding its way into construction projects throughout the region (the average house has 70 tons of sand in it, from its foundation to its roof). The sand is also utilized on ball fields and in parks—most notably, Etowah River sand has been used by the grounds crew at Turner Field, which spreads the light-brown crystals on the Braves' infield in Atlanta. Workers at the operation often pull unusual items from the river bottom: wallets, dentures, and other unmentionables.

MILE 73.9 (34.289883, -84.397981) Riggins Creek & Pine Bluff Landfill. About 1 mile upstream along Riggins Creek is Georgia's largest landfill—Pine Bluff, operated by Waste Management Inc. Each day the landfill accepts around 5,000 tons of municipal and industrial trash and buries it in the ground. Opened in 1993, the facility is expected to reach capacity in 2025. Leachate and runoff from landfills—both contaminants and sediment—can, of course, pollute local streams, and, oh, the waste! Each year, Georgians send to landfills 1.4 million tons of material that could be recycled. The value of that "trash" is estimated at $223 million, including $76 million in plastics and $58 million in aluminum. Waste Management Inc., however, recycles its decomposing trash at Pine Bluff. A pipeline connects methane gas captured at the landfill to the nearby chicken rendering plant on the banks of the Etowah to fuel heating equipment at the facility. Pine Bluff Landfill is nearly 1 mile long and about 0.5 mile wide. Edwards Creek, about 1.5 miles downstream, drains the western half of the facility.

MILE 74.1 (34.288339, -84.400094) Fish Weir.

MILE 75.1 (34.277556, -84.407033) Fish Weir.

MILE 76.6 (34.278725, -84.431158) Fish Weir.

MILE 78.9 (34.268917, -84.432269) Fish Weir.

MILE 80.6 (34.257022, -84.436208) Fish Weir.

MILE 82.3 (34.249247, -84.443081) Sandbar & Strainer. A large sandbar extending from river left restricts the flow of the river to a small channel on river right that can be choked with strainers. Use caution when navigating through this obstacle.

MILE 83 (34.250153, -84.453864) Fish Weir.

MILE 83 (34.250153, -84.453864) Railroad Bridge.

MILE 83.7 (34.251319, -84.465983) Hickory Log Creek & Dam. Several miles upstream from here on Hickory Log Creek sits the most recent effort in "drought-proofing" Metro Atlanta—Hickory Log Dam and Reservoir. Completed in 2010, the 950-foot-wide, 180-foot-high dam on this creek is the largest in Georgia that was not built by the U.S. Army Corps of Engineers or by Georgia Power. Originally estimated to cost $25 million to construct, the project ran over $100 million. The reservoir is considered a pump-storage facility, meaning that water is pumped from the Etowah to fill the reservoir during periods of high flows, and then released as needed to supplement flows when water levels on the Etowah are at their lowest. This scheme ensures adequate river levels just downstream at the City of Canton's water intake pipes. The reservoir is also intended to regulate flows to Lake Allatoona, from which the Cobb-Marietta Water Authority also withdraws water. From its inception, the project has stirred controversy and debate. The state of Alabama filed a lawsuit to stop the project because of concerns about flows being diverted from downstream communities. Within Georgia, water conservation advocates have clashed with dam builders in debates over endangered species, healthy rivers, and the efficient use of state tax dollars for water supplies. Dams, especially in the Upper Etowah River, destroy habitat for federally protected fish like the Etowah, Cherokee, and amber darters, and alter and disrupt natural flows critical to healthy rivers. And the cost of such facilities is astronomical when compared with the cost of conservation measures. Georgia's Environmental Protection Division estimates that conservation and efficiency measures cost from 46¢ to $250 for every 1,000 gallons saved, while building a reservoir can cost $4,000 for every 1,000 gallons. The intake pumps used to fill the reservoir are located just downstream from the creek's mouth, below the I-575 bridge.

WATER INTAKE STRUCTURE FOR HICKORY LOG RESERVOIR IN CANTON, CHEROKEE COUNTY

MILE 84.9 (34.242342, -84.483114) Canton Cotton Mill. This bit of Canton's history stands near the Etowah here. Built in 1924, the massive brick Canton Cotton Mill No. 2 once employed 550 people and processed up to 30,000 bales of cotton each year. Canton is, first and foremost, a mill town with many of the historic mill house neighborhoods still intact. In the 1930s, fully a third of the town's population was employed in the textile industry. This mill operated until 1981, and in 2000 it was transformed into loft apartments. Today no textile industry exists in Canton.

MILE 85.3 (34.240431, -84.487075) Canton Water Intake / City of Canton. Canton was first incorporated under the name of Etowah in 1833, but the following year, the Georgia legislature approved the name Canton. Founders of the town had tried to establish a silk industry as found in Canton, China, and thus wanted a name to promote their pursuits. Though the silk industry never developed, the town ultimately developed a textile industry in its cotton mills. Cherokee County was once among Georgia's top producers of cotton per acre, and Canton Textile Mills, located on the banks of the Etowah, was one of the largest denim manufacturers in the South. Today, Canton is largely a growing bedroom community. In the first decade of the 21st century, Cherokee County consistently ranked among the top

SAND DREDGE, E. CHEROKEE DRIVE, CHEROKEE COUNTY

35 fastest-growing counties in the nation, growing by 51 percent to 214,000. A paddle down the Etowah during a rain reveals the impacts of that growth: expect water the color of the Piedmont's red clay as dirt from the massive land-clearing projects for residential and commercial developments washes into the river from these sites. A muddy river is bad news for fish. The dirt clogs their gills, makes it difficult for them to feed, and decreases their reproductive success. Want to know how it feels to be a fish looking for love in a muddy stream? Try throwing a bucket of mud into your bed! The mud also increases the cost of treating water withdrawn from the river for human consumption, and the Etowah is Canton's sole source—pumped from the river at this site.

MILE 86 (34.236811, -84.497250) Edgewater & Crescent Farm. Atop a high hill on river right here sits Edgewater, the former home of Gus Coggins and his 400-acre Crescent Farm—so named because the Etowah encircled the farm in a crescent shape. Coggins was a successful farmer, horsebreeder, and businessman caught up in the unique social fabric of the post–Civil War South. Because former slaves could be employed more cheaply than white laborers, Coggins, like many businessmen, hired blacks instead of whites. This practice drew the ire of unemployed whites, who began forming vigilante groups to punish white businessmen who hired blacks. The vigilante groups routinely burned Coggins's barns and stables. Historians believe that in response, he constructed a massive stone barn (with materials harvested from the Etowah River) in 1906 to house his best horses. Today what came to be known as the Rock Barn still stands and has been renovated as the home of the Cherokee County Historical Society—a visible reminder of the South's culture of violence and fear in the decades following the Civil War.

MILE 87.5 (34.230900, -84.504461) Canton Wastewater Treatment Plant. Just below the Ga. 5 bridge sits the City of Canton's wastewater treatment plant. This facility can treat 2.35 million gallons of sewage a day. A biological phosphorus removal process along with a chemical addition and filtration allow effluent from this plant to meet requirements of reuse water systems. All water use at the plant itself is from this reuse water. Nevertheless, phosphorus discharges from this and other wastewater treatment plants in the Upper Etowah Basin contribute to high nutrient levels on Lake Allatoona, which can lead to algal blooms and fish kills.

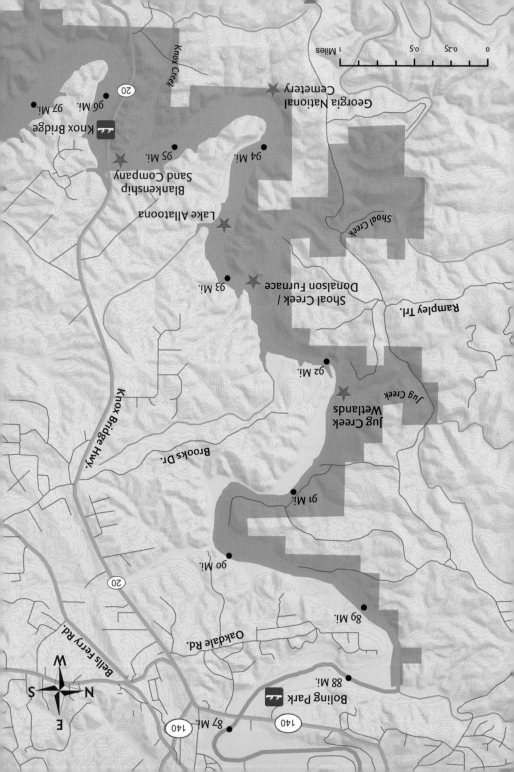

# Lake Allatoona Backwaters

**Length** 8 miles (Boling Park to Knox Bridge)

**Class** I

**Time** 4–7 hours

**Minimum Level** This section can be run any time of the year. It begins in Canton on the flowing river but ends in the backwaters of Lake Allatoona. Water levels on Allatoona vary according to the season and rainfall. Peak levels generally occur in the late spring and early summer, topping out at about 840 feet above mean sea level (MSL). From midsummer to early winter the lake is drawn down to about 823 feet MSL to accommodate heavy rainfall in the winter and early spring.

**River Gauge** Allatoona Lake elevations are posted at http://water.sam.usace.army.mil/actmain.htm#data. River levels in Canton are posted at http://waterdata.usgs.gov/ga/nwis/uv?site_no=02392000.

**Launch Site** There is no developed boat launch in Boling Park, but boats can be launched down the steep riverbank near the riverside picnic tables located between the soccer fields and the tennis courts.

DIRECTIONS The launch is located off Ga. 20 in Canton. From Exit 16 on I-575, travel west on Ga. 20 for 0.7 mile. Turn right at the traffic light onto Ga. 140, cross over the Etowah River, and turn left into Boling Park.

ALLATOONA BACKWATERS, CHEROKEE COUNTY

Take Out Site  The take out is located at the U.S. Army Corps of Engineer Knox Bridge Boat Landing, with ramp and parking area.

DIRECTIONS  From the entrance to Boling Park, turn right onto Ga. 140 (also Ga. 20 at this point). Proceed 0.8 mile and bear right onto Ga. 20 where it splits from Ga. 140. Continue 3.8 miles on Ga. 20 (also Knox Bridge Hwy.) to the Knox Bridge Boat Landing on the left.

Description  A river dies here. Allatoona Dam, some 25 miles downstream from the launch site, transforms the free-flowing Etowah into expansive Lake Allatoona, which has a life of its own. For about 6 miles, a noticeable current persists; that current ceases altogether at Shoal Creek. However, the backwaters of Allatoona provide access to unique natural and historic features, including the wetlands at the mouth of Jug Creek and Donalson Furnace on Shoal Creek.

Outfitters  Lilydipper Outfitters in Canton is the nearest canoe and kayak outfitter.

## Points of Interest

MILE 91.7 (34.237653, -84.537744) Jug Creek Wetlands. On river right where Jug Creek empties into the river is an extensive bottomland wetlands area. When water levels are appropriate, an adventure through this swampy realm is worth the side trip.

MILE 92.8 (34.228850, -84.550619) Shoal Creek / Donalson Furnace. A venture up Shoal Creek on river right leads you about 1 mile to the remains of the Donalson Furnace, a Civil War–era iron furnace. The furnace was built by Judge Joseph Donalson, one of the founders of Canton and the first to build a ferry across the Etowah in Canton. Reportedly, Donalson built the furnace during the war in order to protect his sons from conscription into the Confederate Army. The construction of the iron furnace was a critical part of the war effort and would have exempted his sons from military service. Lending credence to this theory are the facts that the furnace was never fired and that there was no evidence of iron or slag in the area. However, other accounts suggest that Donalson was an ardent financial supporter of the war effort. He was among the largest slaveholders in the county and outfitted an entire company of soldiers in 1861.

MILE 93.5 (34.226658, -84.557236) Lake Allatoona. About 6 miles below Boling Park, you encounter the first backwater sloughs of Lake Allatoona. The river's current slackens, and the river itself spreads over former bottomlands. Some 20 miles downstream, Allatoona Dam blocks the river's path, creating the 12,000-acre impoundment. Completed in 1950 at a cost of $31.5 million, Allatoona Dam's original primary purpose was to save the city of Rome downstream from routine flooding. Now, the federal impoundment does much more. The powerhouse at the dam produces enough electricity to power 17,000 homes, and the recreation-tourism industry that hosts 6 million lake visitors each year generates an estimated $93 million annually. The lake also enables one of the biggest controversies in Georgia's water management policy—an interbasin water transfer from the Etowah to the Chattahoochee basin. Each day, the Cobb-Marietta Water Authority withdraws

SAND DREDGE, CHEROKEE COUNTY

millions of gallons from Lake Allatoona and pumps it to water users in the Chattahoochee basin. Much of that withdrawal is never returned to the Etowah, depriving the lake and downstream communities of the benefit of that water. In part, it was the threat of water transfers to Atlanta, out of the Coosa River basin, which flows into Alabama, that prompted the state of Alabama to file suit in 1990 to stop Atlanta's effort to take more water from the Chattahoochee and the Etowah Rivers. That lawsuit evolved into a water war that remains unresolved. Lake Allatoona itself has long suffered from poor water quality as a result of rapid land development and stormwater runoff in its 1,110-square-mile watershed. Nutrients, primarily phosphorus, have resulted in algal blooms on the lake that can lead to fish kills.

MILE 94.4 (34.231028, -84.571458) Georgia National Cemetery. On river right here overlooking the Etowah is the 775-acre Georgia National Cemetery, the second national cemetery in Georgia. The Georgia National Cemetery opened for burials on April 24, 2006, and was dedicated that June. It includes sites for 33,000 full-casket graves, 3,000 in-ground sites for cremation remains, and 3,000 columbarium niches for cremation remains. The property was donated by the late Scott Hudgens, a well-known Atlanta land developer who was a World War II veteran.

MILE 95.5 (34.216478, -84.564606) Blankenship Sand Co. Blankenship Sand Company operates a sand dredge in the stretch of lake above and below Knox Bridge. The company also operates a dredge upstream near East Cherokee Drive (near mile 72). Here they suck sand from the river bottom, helping to prevent the lake from filling with sediment—a process that is inevitable. Each year, Blankenship and his crew remove about 100,000 tons of sand from the river—enough to fill 4,000 tractor trailers. That 100,000 tons of sand represents 15 million gallons of storage capacity on the lake. Sand dredges are common on all Georgia rivers, but Blankenship is the only operator on the length of the Etowah.

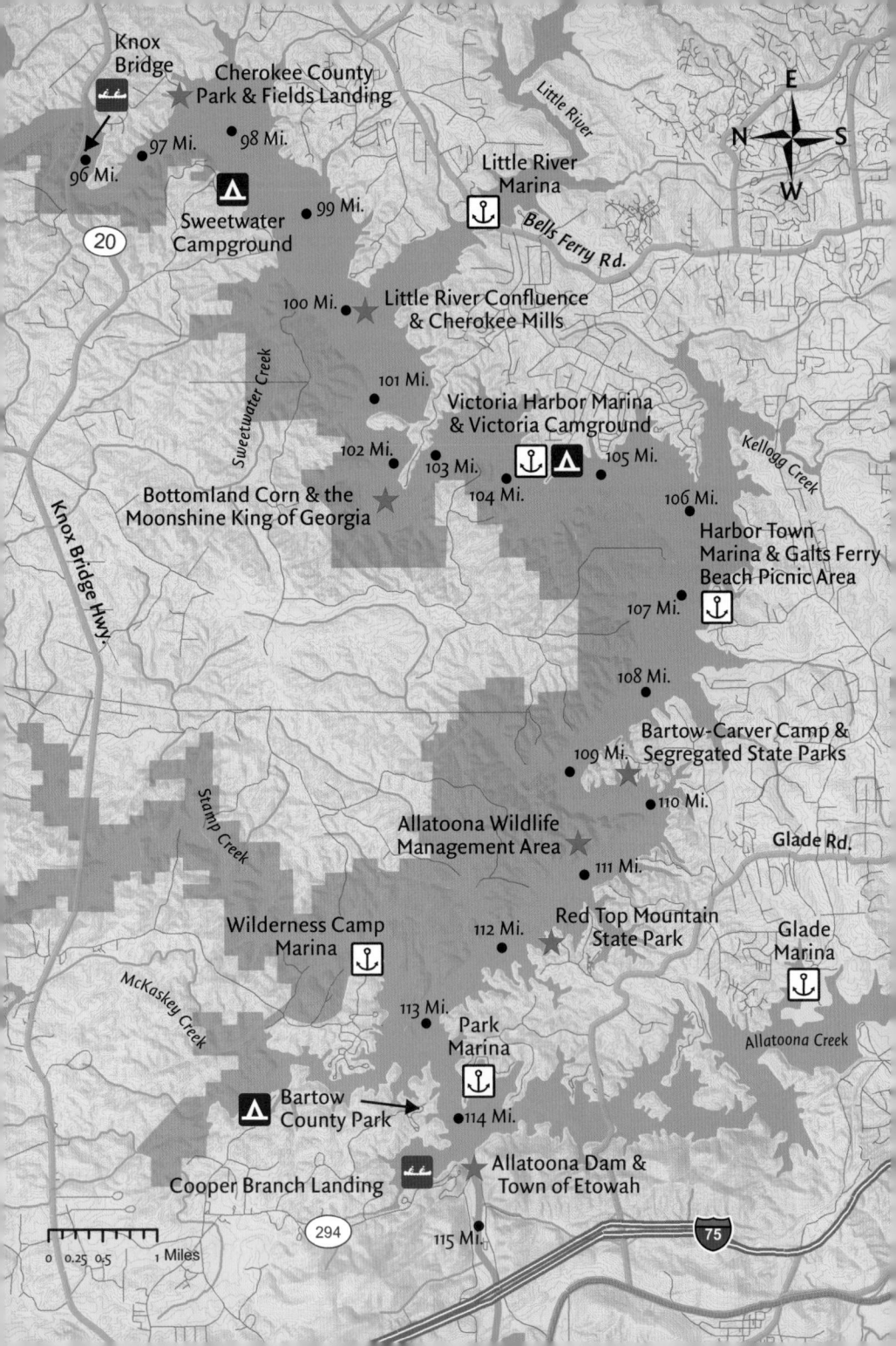

Knox
Bridge

Cherokee County
Park & Fields Landing

97 Mi.    98 Mi.

96 Mi.

20

Sweetwater
Campground

99 Mi.

Little River

Little River
Marina

Bells Ferry Rd.

E
N    S
W

100 Mi.    Little River Confluence
& Cherokee Mills

Sweetwater Creek

101 Mi.

Victoria Harbor Marina
& Victoria Camground

102 Mi.    103 Mi.    105 Mi.

104 Mi.    106 Mi.

Kellogg Creek

Bottomland Corn & the
Moonshine King of Georgia

Harbor Town
Marina & Galts Ferry
Beach Picnic Area

Knox Bridge Hwy.

107 Mi.

108 Mi.

Bartow-Carver Camp &
Segregated State Parks

109 Mi.

110 Mi.

Stamp Creek

Allatoona Wildlife
Management Area

Glade Rd.

111 Mi.

Wilderness Camp
Marina

Red Top Mountain
State Park

Glade
Marina

112 Mi.

McKaskey Creek

Allatoona Creek

113 Mi.

Park
Marina

Bartow
County Park

114 Mi.

Cooper Branch Landing

294

Allatoona Dam &
Town of Etowah

115 Mi.

75

0   0.25  0.5        1 Miles

# Lake Allatoona

**Length** 17 miles (Knox Bridge to Allatoona Dam)

**Class** 1

**Time** 9+ hours

**Minimum Level** This section is wholly on Lake Allatoona and can be run at any time of the year. Water levels on Allatoona vary according to the season and rainfall. Peak levels generally occur in the late spring and early summer, topping out at about 840 feet above mean sea level (MSL). From midsummer to early winter the lake is drawn down to about 823 feet MSL to accommodate heavy rainfall in the winter and early spring.

---

**River Gauge** Allatoona Lake elevations are posted at http://water.sam.usace.army.mil/actmain.htm#data.

**Launch Site** A large concrete boat ramp and paved parking area are located at Knox Bridge on Ga. 20, 5.5 miles west of Canton.

DIRECTIONS The launch is located between Cartersville and Canton on Ga. 20. From I-75 at Exit 290, take Ga. 20 East (Knox Bridge Hwy.) toward Canton, traveling 12 miles to the Knox Bridge boat ramp on the right.

**Take Out Site** There are multiple access points on Lake Allatoona, which is a reservoir operated by the U.S. Army Corps of Engineers. Lake users can create many trips utilizing campgrounds and boat ramps as well as local and state parks. On the mainstem of the river are nine boat landings in the 17 miles from Knox Bridge to Allatoona Dam.

**Description** With more than 12,000 acres and an estimated 270 miles of shoreline, Lake Allatoona offers almost limitless exploration opportunities. Of course, if you are in a person-powered vessel, you have to work for every mile: there is no current to push you along. Despite the lake's location in the burgeoning suburbs of north Metro Atlanta, its northern shoreline is surprisingly undeveloped, with 9,300 acres protected as a state wildlife management area. Beneath the lake's expansive waters is a landscape rich in history.

**Outfitters** Several private marinas operate on the lake, including

- Little River Marina located on the Little River is a full-service marina with boat launch and docks, ship's store, restaurant, and powerboat rentals: 6986 Bells Ferry Rd., Canton, Ga. 30114, (770) 345-2900, www.littlerivermarina.com

- Victoria Harbor Marina on the mainstem of the Etowah is a full-service marina with boat launch and docks, ship's store, groceries, restaurant, and powerboat rentals: 1000 Victoria Landing, Woodstock, Ga. 30189, (770) 926-7718, www.bestinboating.com/victoria

- Harbor Town Marina on the mainstem of the Etowah is a full-service marina with boat launch and docks, ship's store, restaurant, and powerboat rentals: 7370 Galts Ferry Rd., Acworth, Ga. 30102, (770) 974-6422, www.bestinboating .com/harbor

- Park Marina on the mainstem of the Etowah is full-service marina located within Red Top Mountain State Park with boat launch and docks, ship's store, and powerboat rentals: 651 Park Marina Road, Cartersville, Ga. 30121, (770) 974-2628, www.bestinboating.com/allatoona

- Wilderness Camp Marina located just off the mainstem of the river on Stamp Creek offers boat launch and docks and groceries: 451 Wilderness Camp Rd., White, Ga. 30184, (770) 386-2170

- Glade Marina located on Allatoona Creek provides boat launch and docks and restaurants: 5400 Kings Camp Rd., Acworth, Ga. 30102, (770) 975-7000, www .glademarina.com

- Holiday Marina located on Allatoona Creek is a full-service marina with boat launch and docks, ship's store, groceries, restaurant, cabin rentals and canoe, kayak, and powerboat rentals: 5989 Groovers Landing, Acworth, Ga. 30102, (770) 974-2575, www.lakeallatoona.net

Other outfitters offering canoe and kayak rentals include Lilydipper's in Canton and Euharlee Creek Outfitters in Euharlee.

## Points of Interest

MILE 97.4 (34.201783, -84.561639) Cherokee County Park & Fields Landing. Operated by the county, this small park offers picnic tables, playground, horseshoe court, fishing dock, boat ramp, and portable toilets. It is also where one of Cherokee County's most successful early settlers lived. Jeremiah Field, already a successful planter and landowner in South Carolina, moved to the county around 1833 and settled in this area with his wife and six children. He farmed and operated a gristmill here. The 1850 census shows that he owned 39 slaves and that his property was valued at $50,000, making him the wealthiest man in the county. He and his family are buried across the lake in the Fields Chapel Methodist Church Cemetery.

MILE 98.6 (34.193392, -84.576044) Sweetwater Campground. A U.S. Army Corps of Engineers campground, the facility boasts of 151 campsites, hot showers, coin laundry, restrooms, beach, and boat ramp.

MILE 100.1 (34.178008, -84.594967) Little River Confluence & Cherokee Mills. Approximately 1 mile upstream on the Little River once stood Cherokee Mills, a gristmill, sawmill, and later a cotton gin. In the 1830s the first dam and mill were erected at the site, operating well into the 20th century. Imagine if you will the scene on the Little each fall when cotton was ginned at the mill. It was said that operators dumped into the river mounds of the fluffy white seeds that had been removed by the gin, undoubtedly creating a floating mass of white from the mill to the Etowah and beyond. The old mill site is now underwater. Little River Marina extends over the approximate location of the mill.

MILE 102.4 (34.175294, -84.624647) Bottomland Corn & the Moonshine King of Georgia. In this vicinity, the water of Lake Allatoona now covers the bottomland once farmed by John Henry Hardin, a man known as the Moonshine King of Georgia. The distillation of liquor was commonly practiced by farmers throughout the Southern Appalachians. The legend of the "King" suggests that the impetus for his entrance into the business was the temperamental Etowah, which regularly overflowed into Hardin's cornfields, spoiling his crop. During one monumental flood in the 1910s, a farmhand suggested to Hardin that the crop might yet still be suitable for the production of whiskey. Whether the legend is true or not, by 1917, state and federal authorities had indicted Hardin on liquor charges. Before he died in 1943, 19 cases had been brought against him. Yet for all his trouble with the law, he was widely respected for his honesty and integrity in the community. He employed more than 100 workers at the peak of his moonshine empire while serving as a deacon at nearby Sixes Methodist Church, where he also taught Sunday school and led singing. His life took a tragic turn in the summer of 1932. That year his son, Paul Henry, who worked in the family business, was arrested on serious federal charges. Out of jail on $3,000 bond, he began drinking heavily. On June 19, he shot and killed his young wife and their four children before turning the gun on himself. It is said that John Henry never recovered from the horrific tragedy. Multiple arrests, prison sentences, fines, and the seizure of property by the government left him nearly penniless at the time of his death.

MILE 104.1 (34.155589, -84.622128) Victoria Harbor Marina & Victoria Campground. Find here a private marina and adjacent U.S. Army Corps of Engineers campground. The campground features 72 campsites (all with electric and water hookups), hot showers, restrooms, coin laundry facility, public swimming beach, and boat ramp.

LAKE ALLATOONA, CHEROKEE COUNTY

**MILE 106.6 (34.134200, -84.642047)** Harbor Town Marina & Galts Ferry Beach Picnic Area. This private marina is adjacent to a U.S. Army Corps of Engineers public day use area. One of the lake's more popular day use areas, Galts Ferry features a large beach and swimming area, picnic shelters, restrooms, and boat ramp.

**MILE 109.7 (34.142800, -84.669669)** Bartow-Carver Camp & Segregated State Parks. In the separate-but-equal days of the segregated South, what is now Bartow-Carver Camp was George Washington Carver State Park—established in 1950 as the state's first "park for Negroes." John Atkinson, a black man from Atlanta, arranged to lease the property from the U.S. Army Corps of Engineers for a private, blacks-only resort, but Bartow County refused him a license to run such an establishment. Feeling the heat of mounting protests from black veterans of World War II, Governor Herman Eugene Talmadge then offered to make the facility a "State Park for Negroes." It remained a state park until 1975, when

Bartow County took over the lease and operation of facilities. During its 25 years as Carver State Park, it was also a performance venue, with Ray Charles and Little Richard among the entertainers who appeared there. Future Atlanta mayor Andrew Young and his family frequently waterskied there, and Coretta Scott King and her children also visited. The park now features two rental facilities for group events. The facilities and other amenities (including the beach) are open only to those renting the facilities, although there is no fee to use the boat ramp.

MILE 110.8 (34.147850, -84.680542) Allatoona Wildlife Management Area. Allatoona's undeveloped north shore owes its wildness to its protection as the Allatoona Wildlife Management Area. The 9,300-acre WMA stretches 14 miles along the Etowah's course through the lake, providing opportunities for hunting, hiking, and a host of other activities. It also provides a stark contrast to the lake's southern shore, some of which is heavily developed.

MILE 111.6 (34.154700, -84.692014) Red Top Mountain State Park. This 1,776-acre state park features 12 miles of hiking trails, 4 miles of cycling trails, rental cottages, an RV campground, primitive camping, and even a yurt, but due to budget constraints the 33-room lodge closed in 2010. The mountain and park derives its name from the rich red color of the soil caused by the high iron-ore content.

MILE 113.9 (34.167358, -84.721108) Bartow County Park. Operated by the Bartow County Recreation Department, this park includes picnic areas, playground, campground, restrooms, showers, boat ramp, and beach.

MILE 114.3 (34.169378, -84.729111) Cooper Branch Landing. Closest to Allatoona Dam, this boat ramp is located 0.2 mile from the dam in the slough to the north. Operated by the U.S. Army Corps of Engineers, the park offers picnic tables and restrooms.

MILE 114.4 (34.163239, -84.729044) Allatoona Dam & Town of Etowah. At the deepest portion of the lake near the dam sit the remains of the town of Etowah—founded in the early 1840s around the Cooper Iron Works by Mark Anthony Cooper and others. Etowah's founders utilized water power from the Etowah and the locally abundant iron ore deposits to create a mining and manufacturing center. At its heyday in the late 1850s as a thriving, backwoods industrial complex, the town had a workforce of 600 that was serviced by a school, church, boardinghouse, bordello, bank, post office, and brewery. The town produced railroad tracks from the iron ore extracted from nearby hills, and the flour mill produced up to 300 barrels of flour a day. Cooper sold the land to investors in 1862 and turned a tidy profit, which he then invested in the Confederacy, ultimately losing his entire fortune by the war's end. The town of Etowah thrived until 1864, when it was destroyed by Union forces during the Civil War. After the war, the town was never rebuilt. Today, the town's remains, with the exception of the furnace

ALLATOONA DAM, BARTOW COUNTY

located near the base of the dam, lie beneath the water of Lake Allatoona. Except for Canton's brief flirtation with the name of Etowah, this is the only settlement to ever bear the name of the river. The Indian word Etowah has never been successfully translated, thus historians do not know what, if any significance or meaning, is attached to the name.

# Indian Mounds

Length 10.5 miles (Base of Allatoona Dam to Henry Floyd's)

Class 1

Time 4–6 hours

Minimum Level The river here can be run year round, but releases from the Allatoona Dam can create unsafe conditions. Paddlers should use caution when paddling this section during hydropower releases, which cause rapid rises in water levels. Release schedules are issued by the U.S. Army Corps of Engineers daily at midnight and can be retrieved by calling (706) 334-7213.

ARROWHEAD FOUND ON ETOWAH RIVER, BARTOW COUNTY

River Gauge Etowah River at Allatoona Dam http://waterdata.usgs.gov/nwis /uv?site_no=02394000.

Launch Site A large concrete boat ramp and paved parking area are located at the launch site near Allatoona Dam. Toilet facilities are in a nearby day-use recreation area.

DIRECTIONS From I-75, take Exit 401 (Red Top Mountain Rd.) Travel west for 0.5 mile. Turn right onto U.S. 41 and travel 1 mile. Turn right onto Allatoona Dam Road, and travel 1 mile to the entrance to the boat ramp on the left.

Take Out Site Henry Floyd, who also owns Ladd's Farm Supply in Cartersville, makes this private land available for public use. Amenities include boat ramp, shelters and swings overlooking the river. The road and parking area are gravel.

DIRECTIONS From Main Street in Cartersville, travel west on Main Street (Ga. 113 and Ga. 61) for 2.5 miles. Turn right onto Euharlee Road and travel 1 mile to a gravel road on the left. Turn left and follow road to the river and the boat ramp.

Description Starting in the shadow of Allatoona Dam, this 10-mile section takes you from 20th-century engineering (Allatoona Dam) to precolonial engineering (Etowah Indian Mounds and Fish Weir). Owing to Allatoona Dam and the cold, clear water it issues from the bottom of the lake, the water appears pristine and inviting. Shoals and rapids are limited to Native American fish weirs and small ripples, and there are no obstacles exceeding Class I in difficulty. The lone hazard is the historic Thompson Weinman Dam, a lowhead dam that must be portaged.

BELOW ALLATOONA DAM, BARTOW COUNTY

**Outfitters** Euharlee Creek Outfitters in Euharlee is the nearest canoe and kayak outfitter.

## Points of Interest

MILE 114.4 (34.163239, -84.729044) **Allatoona Dam.** Located 1 mile upstream from the launch, Allatoona Dam was constructed by the U.S. Army Corps of Engineers in the 1940s and became fully operational in 1950. Although it was built, in large part, to prevent flooding in downstream communities, particularly Rome, it serves multiple purposes, including hydroelectric power generation, water supply, recreation, and fish and wildlife management. While the river looks clean and pure here, the dam and its operation have altered flow regimes, water temperature, and oxygen levels in the Lower Etowah. As a result, native freshwater mussel species have vanished from the Lower Etowah. Also, fish species have declined from a predam diversity of 80 species to an estimated 45 species today.

MILE 117.3 (34.154281, -84.770792) **Bridge Pilings.** These pillars are all that remains of the Western and Atlantic Railroad bridge, which was completed in the 1840s by Cherokee Indian laborers. During the Civil War, in late May 1864 the span was burned by retreating Confederate forces as Sherman's troops advanced to the western end of Allatoona Mountain during the Atlanta Campaign. Union

troops rebuilt the bridge in six days, continuing their march to Atlanta. Trains passed over these stone structures into the 1940s, when the line was abandoned and a new bridge was constructed just downstream.

MILE 118.4 (34.145364, -84.783506) Thompson Weinman Dam. This lowhead dam dating from the early 1900s provided Cartersville's first electricity and powered local industry until the late 20th century. The industrial complex adjacent to it is Chemical Products Corp., which processes barite. Found in abundance in the Cartersville area, this mineral was mined on the south bank of the river on the hills above the portage route for more than a century. It is used in the manufacture of paper, glass, and rubber. The rich, white pigment made from crushed barite is used in radiology to accompany X-rays of the digestive system. The brick building next to the dam is the old City of Cartersville waterworks. The city now withdraws its drinking water supply directly from Lake Allatoona.

MILE 119.8 (34.130011, -84.797933) Riverfront Development & Bank Erosion. Owners of the homes lining the riverbank here are engaged in an ongoing battle with Mother Nature and, by extension, with the U.S. Army Corps of Engineers, which controls Mother Nature (to the extent that it regulates the flow from Allatoona Dam). The powerful releases for hydroelectric generation at the dam ac-

THOMPSON WEINMAN DAM IN CARTERSVILLE, BARTOW COUNTY

INDIAN MOUNDS

celerate the natural process of bank erosion. As a result, many homeowners are literally losing their backyards. Many have constructed walls to prevent this erosion—with permission from the Corps and the state of Georgia—a solution that eliminates important riparian habitat and contributes to accelerated erosion of adjacent property. When Allatoona Dam was constructed in the 1940s, the corps purchased "sloughage easements" from downstream riverfront property owners, knowing that operation of the dam would "take" property. This program is no longer in place; it is unlikely that the corps would purchase the pricy homes and property that now stand where farm fields once spread.

MILE 119.9 (34.130133, -84.797369) Fish Weir.

MILE 120.4 (34.123967, -84.805772) Etowah Indian Mounds & Fish Weir. Home to several thousand Native Americans between AD 1000 and AD 1550, this 54-acre site contains six earthen mounds, a plaza, village area, borrow pits, and defensive ditch. This is the most intact Mississippian Culture site in the southeastern United States. The mounds are at river right just opposite the confluence of Pumpkinvine Creek. The tallest mound rises 63 feet above the former village site. During the Civil War, Union general William Sherman climbed to the top of this

WATERFORD SUBDIVISION IN CARTERSVILLE BELOW
ALLATOONA DAM, BARTOW COUNTY

INDIAN MOUNDS

mound, only to be fired upon by Confederate canons across the river. The site can be accessed from the river only by prior arrangement with Georgia Department of Natural Resources resource managers at the site. Additional mounds were once located across the river along Pumpkinvine Creek, but those mounds have been destroyed. A fish weir bisects the river near the mouth of the creek.

MILE 120.8 (34.121772, -84.810497) Fish Weir.

MILE 121.4 (34.120289, -84.819472) Douthit's Ferry. Early pioneer James Douthit once operated a ferry near this location and lends his name to the modern-day Douthit's Ferry Road. The iron-truss bridge still standing here was built in 1886, atop the same rock piers that supported a wooden bridge that put Douthit out of the ferrying business prior to the Civil War. During the war, the bridge was destroyed and Douthit briefly returned to ferrying until a new wooden bridge was built shortly after the war.

MILE 123.2 (34.130728, -84.846208) Cartersville Airport. At this bend in the river, you are at the northern edge of the airport runway. Don't be surprised to see low-flying aircraft.

MILE 123.7 (34.137764, -84.841264) Pettit Creek & Leake Site. Prior to the 1940s, on river left opposite the mouth of Pettit Creek, stood three Indian mounds. They were razed and used for road fill when Ga. Hwy. 113 was constructed at its present location. Archaeologist who have excavated the remains of the mounds

FISH WEIR AT INDIAN MOUNDS, BARTOW COUNTY

suggest that human habitation of the site began in 300 BC. It was abandoned around AD 650.

MILE 124.5 (34.148181, -84.843206) Fish Weir.

MILE 125 (34.148714, -84.849906) Fish Weir. Though not distinct at river level, this weir is clearly visible in aerial photographs. The weirs on the Etowah vary in quality and preservation. Some were breached for navigational purposes, while others were improved and are maintained.

FISH WEIR NEAR GA. 113, BARTOW COUNTY

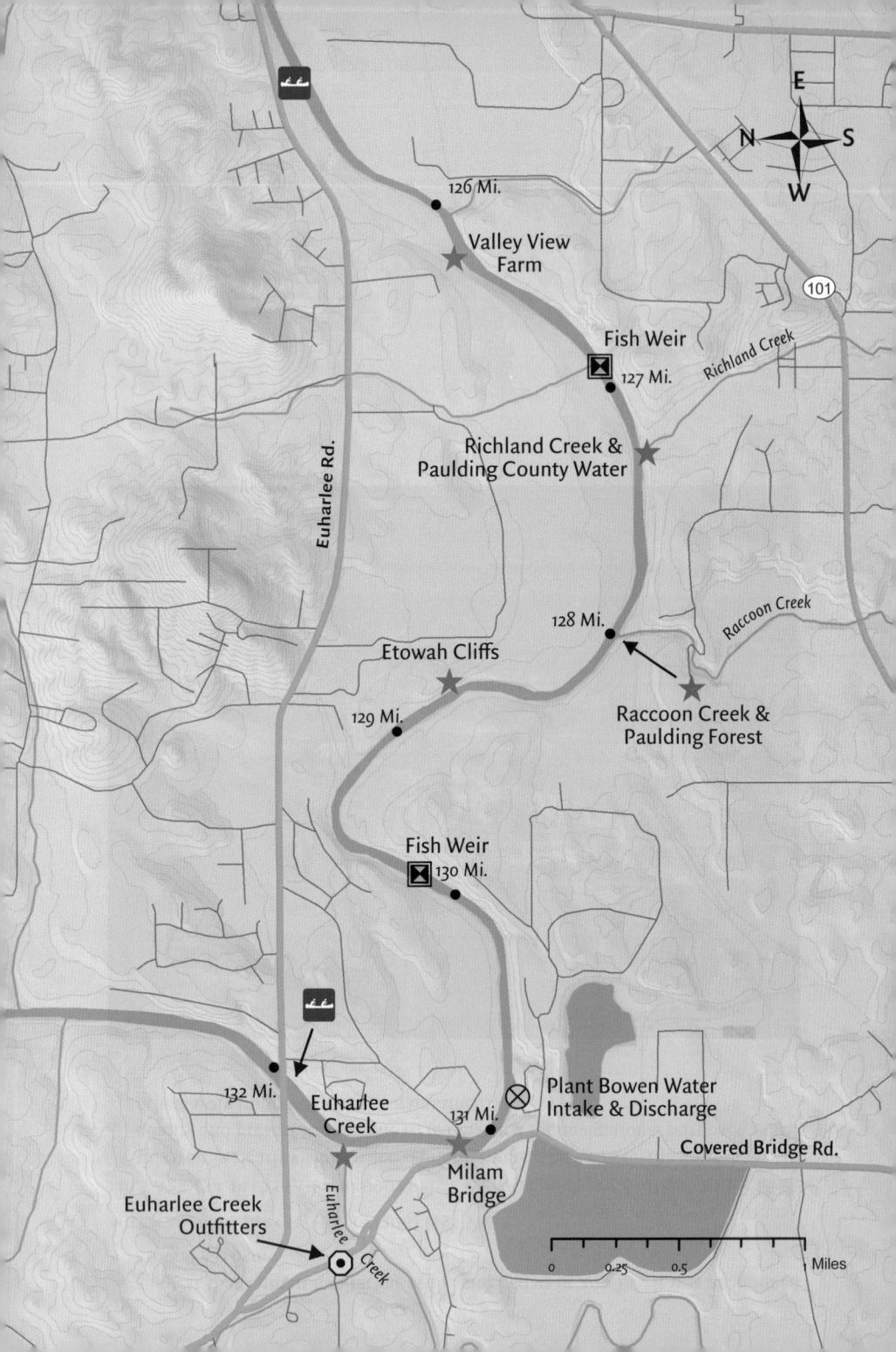

# Euharlee

Length  7 miles (Henry Floyd's to Euharlee Road)

Class  I

Time  3–5 hours

Minimum Level  The river here can be run year round, but releases from the Allatoona Dam can create unsafe conditions. Paddlers should use caution when paddling this section during hydropower releases, which cause rapid rises in water levels. Release schedules are issued by the U.S. Army Corps of Engineers daily at midnight and can be retrieved by calling (706) 334-7213.

River Gauge  Etowah River at Allatoona Dam http://waterdata.usgs.gov/nwis /uv?02394000.

---

Launch Site  Henry Floyd, who also owns Ladd's Farm Supply in Cartersville, makes this private land available for public use. Amenities include a boat ramp, shelters, and swings overlooking the river. The road and parking area are gravel.

DIRECTIONS  From Main Street in Cartersville, travel west on Main Street (Ga. 113 and Ga. 61) for 2.5 miles. Turn right onto Euharlee Road and travel 1 mile to a gravel road. Turn left and follow the gravel road to the river and boat ramp.

Take Out Site  This boat ramp is located beneath the Euharlee Road Bridge and is suitable for launching canoe, kayaks, and small motorized craft. The property is owned by the City of Euharlee, which is developing a riverfront park here. A small parking area is available.

DIRECTIONS  From the Henry Floyd property, travel west on Euharlee Road for 4 miles. Turn left onto Dobson Drive. The parking area and boat launch are on the immediate right.

Description  This 7-mile section takes you through Bartow's County's plantation row. Prior to the Civil War, several plantation homes lined the Etowah here, though today only one (Valley View) remains. The trip also takes you past Georgia Power Co.'s Plant Bowen, one of the largest coal-fired power plants in the country. Though the cooling towers and pollution-control stacks loom on the horizon, the route is primarily peaceful and rural with some residential riverfront development. Shoals and rapids are limited to Native American fish weirs and small ripples. No obstacles exceed Class I in difficulty.

Outfitters  Euharlee Creek Outfitters in Euharlee is the nearest canoe and kayak outfitter.

## Points of Interest

MILE 126.3 (34.137664, -84.865808) Valley View Farm. Not visible from the river, this circa 1848 antebellum plantation home built by James Caldwell Sproull sits on a knoll overlooking rolling pastures and the Etowah. The walls of the Greek Revival–style house are 3 feet thick, with the brick made on location by slaves— their fingerprints are still visible on some of the bricks. When the Civil War threatened their home, the Sproulls fled to Alabama. Following the Battle of Atlanta, Union general John Schofield occupied the house for about three months. Officers used the second floor for living quarters, but the parlor was used as a stable for horses and the piano was used as a trough (the horses were brought into the house because Confederate snipers were shooting them). The names of two Union soldiers scribbled on the walls are still visible in an upstairs closet.

When the Sproull family returned to the farm from Alabama, they came via river vessel from downstream on the Etowah and Coosa Rivers from Rome. The home has remained in the family since its construction—ownership that now spans five generations—and is on the National Register of Historic Places.

VALLEY VIEW FARM, BARTOW COUNTY

MILE 126.9 (34.129928, -84.873156) Fish Weir. A careful examination of the mouth of this weir reveals wooden structures that were added to the original rock structure.

MILE 127.3 (34.127650, -84.877033) Richland Creek & Paulding County Water. This tributary at river left drains portions of fast-growing Paulding County, whose civic leaders plan to build a water supply reservoir on the creek that would be filled with water pumped from the Etowah River. Paulding County currently purchases most of its water from neighboring Cobb County, which withdraws water from Lake Allatoona 10 miles upstream.

MILE 128 (34.127764, -84.890633) Raccoon Creek & Paulding Forest. The headwaters of this tributary at river left are protected as part of the 6,500-acre Paulding Forest, making Raccoon Creek one of the few streams below Allatoona

EUHARLEE CREEK, BARTOW COUNTY

EUHARLEE

FISH WEIR IN BARTOW COUNTY WITH PLANT BOWEN

Dam that supports healthy populations of the federally protected Cherokee and Etowah darters. Restoration projects on this stream directed by the Nature Conservancy aim to improve habitat and expand populations of these rare fish, which are found only in the Etowah River basin—and nowhere else in the world.

MILE 128.7 (34.137925, -84.894864) Etowah Cliffs. On river right atop the high bluff here once stood Etowah Cliffs, the antebellum plantation home of William Henry Stiles, a former U.S. congressman from Savannah. Stiles built the home as a summer retreat to escape the Georgia coast but eventually moved to the home in the 1830s. Juliette Gordon Lowe, founder of the Girl Scouts and a relative of the Stileses, visited the home as a child and swam in the river here. At the base of the bluff are several clear, cold springs.

MILE 129.8 (34.140019, -84.906967) Fish Weir. One of the most impressive weirs on the Etowah. This double V stretches dramatically across the river. Small openings in the weir offer several possible passages—the best being on river left.

MILE 130.8 (34.134564, -84.921692) Plant Bowen Water Intake & Discharge. Among the largest coal-fired electric generating facilities in the country, Plant Bowen produces 20 percent of the electricity that Georgia Power sells. The facility utilizes about 40 million gallons of water each day from the Etowah—about half of which is returned to the river after use with the temperature slightly el-

ETOWAH NEAR EUHARLEE, BARTOW COUNTY

evated. You can feel the temperature difference as you paddle past the plant's discharge. This water is used to cool the plant's system—converting steam to water so that the water can be heated again to produce the steam that turns turbines that produce electricity. The water that is not returned to the river is lost in the cooling process. The large white plumes of "smoke" emerging from the cylindrical cooling towers are actually water vapor. It takes tremendous amounts of water to produce the electricity we depend upon. In fact, more water is used to produce energy in Georgia than is used for any other single purpose—including agriculture.

MILE 131.2 (34.137670, -84.924822) Milam Bridge. The rock piers of this iron-truss bridge predate the Civil War and supported a wooden bridge crossed by thousands of Union and Confederate troops. Locally, the iron bridge is infamously known as the site of the discovery of the grisly murder of a 12-year-old girl in the 1950s. Her body was bound in chains and thrown into the river here. The murderer was sentenced to death—the last person from Bartow County to die in the state's electric chair.

MILE 131.5 (34.144067, -84.924842) Euharlee Creek. About 0.4 mile up Euharlee Creek are the Euharlee Creek Covered Bridge and the town of Euharlee. Built in 1886 by Washington King, son of freed slave and notable bridge builder Horace King, the bridge was in use until 1976. The remains of a gristmill dating to the 1840s can be seen just downstream of the bridge. This gristmill fueled the area's first population boom, and in 1852 the settlement known as Burgess Mill incorporated as Euharleeville. Residents dropped the "ville" in 1870. The Indian word Euharlee means "she laughs as she runs." Since the early 1990s, Euharlee has experienced unprecedented growth, and this sleepy hamlet has grown into a large bedroom community for surrounding urban centers.

EUHARLEE CREEK, BARTOW COUNTY

EUHARLEE

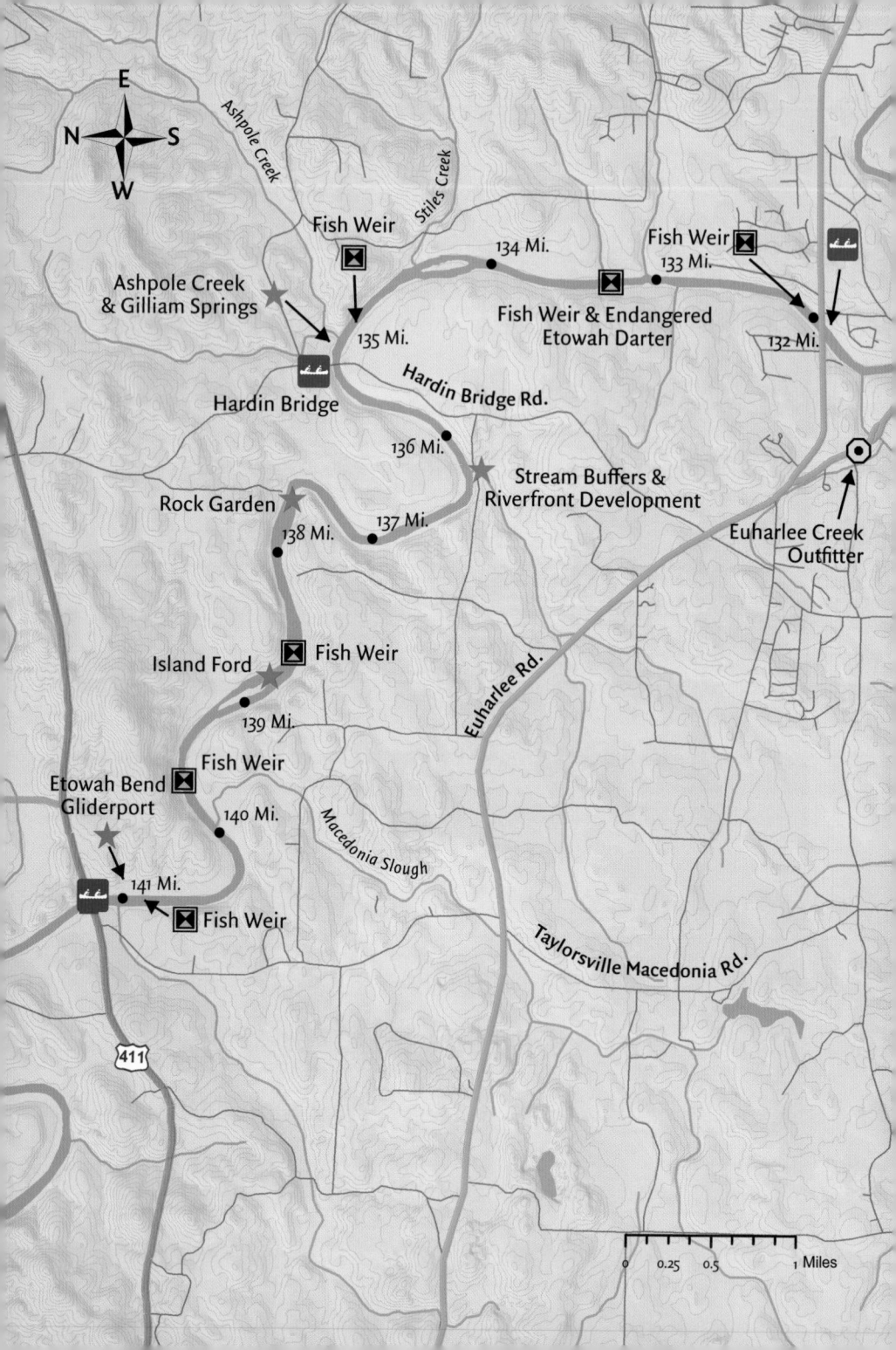

Ashpole Creek

Stiles Creek

**Fish Weir**

134 Mi.

**Fish Weir**

133 Mi.

Ashpole Creek
& Gilliam Springs

**Fish Weir & Endangered
Etowah Darter**

132 Mi.

135 Mi.

**Hardin Bridge**

Hardin Bridge Rd.

**Euharlee Creek
Outfitter**

136 Mi.

**Stream Buffers &
Riverfront Development**

**Rock Garden**

138 Mi.

137 Mi.

Euharlee Rd.

**Island Ford**

**Fish Weir**

139 Mi.

**Fish Weir**

**Etowah Bend
Gliderport**

140 Mi.

Macedonia Slough

141 Mi.

**Fish Weir**

Taylorsville Macedonia Rd.

411

0    0.25    0.5    1 Miles

# Hardin Bridge

Length  9 miles (Euharlee Road to U.S. 411)

Class  1

Time  4–6 hours

Minimum Level  The river here can be run year round. Releases from the Allatoona Dam can cause water levels to fluctuate dramatically. Paddlers should use caution when paddling this section during hydropower releases, which cause rapid rises in water levels. Release schedules are issued by the U.S. Army Corps of Engineers daily at midnight and can be retrieved by calling (706) 334-7213.

River Gauge  The nearest river gauge is located at the take out at U.S. 411 near Kingston: http://waterdata.usgs.gov/ga/nwis/uv?site_no=02395000.

Launch Site  A boat ramp and parking area were developed by Bartow County and the City of Euharlee at Euharlee Road in 2011. The City of Euharlee plans to develop a riverside park at the location as well.

DIRECTIONS  From Main Street in Cartersville, travel west on Main Street (Ga. 113 and Ga. 61) for 2.5 miles. Turn right onto Euharlee Road and travel 5 miles. Turn left onto Dobson Drive; the entrance to the boat ramp parking area is immediately on the right.

Take Out Site  Currently, the best take out is an undeveloped slope at the southeast corner of the U.S. 411 bridge. Most vehicles can access a road that leads to the top of this slope beneath the bridge. This is an extremely steep take out location. A boat ramp at the southwest corner of the U.S. 411 bridge is planned.

DIRECTIONS  From the Euharlee Road launch site off Dobson Drive, turn left onto Euharlee Road and proceed for 4.3 miles. Turn right onto Taylorsville Macedonia Road and proceed 2.5 miles. Turn right onto U.S. 411. Immediately cross the bridge over the Etowah, and then turn right onto a gravel drive located on the east side of the bridge. Follow the gravel drive up the hill and down to the river to the take out site.

Description  This 9-mile section may be the most scenic and popular paddle on the Etowah River in Bartow County. The paddle path crosses no less than six Native American fish weirs and winds beneath riverside bluffs. The highlight is a 0.2-mile rock garden followed by a series of islands and shoals. With many places to stop and play, this is a favorite paddle for families. Some residential development encroaches on the river in places, but the river maintains a rural feel. Obstacles are limited to Native American fish weirs and small shoals and do not exceed Class 1 in difficulty.

Outfitters Euharlee Creek Outfitters in Euharlee and the Coosa River Basin Initiative in Rome are the nearest canoe and kayak outfitters.

## Points of Interest

MILE 132.1 (34.148522, -84.920050) Fish Weir. This weir is visible from the Euharlee Road bridge during low water. If the shoal is visible, then the remainder of the fish weirs on this stretch are also visible.

MILE 133.3 (34.165822, -84.916703) Fish Weir & Endangered Etowah Darter. Shoals like this one created by this Native American fish weir are the preferred habitat of many fish, including the federally endangered Etowah darter. This fish is still found in the Upper Etowah and its tributaries, although before the construction of Allatoona Dam in 1950 it was also found in the river below Allatoona Pass. The operation of the dam has dramatically altered habitat in the river's 48 miles from the dam to Rome. Prior to the dam's construction, 80 species of fish could be found in this stretch of river. Today, only 45 species exist here. However, there is hope. Biologists believe that by altering the operation of Allatoona Dam, it may be possible to restore some species to the mainstem of the Etowah, including the Etowah darter.

MILE 134.9 (34.187111, -84.920725) Fish Weir.

MILE 135 (34.188156, -84.922167) Ashpole Creek & Gilliam Springs. Paddle into the mouth of Ashpole Creek with your hand in the water to note the decided change in water temperature. About 0.1 mile upstream on Ashpole Creek is the spring run from Gilliam Springs—a beautiful clear, strong spring that issues forth from the rock wall about 8 feet high. It is accessible by walking up the creek. During the summer months, large numbers of striped bass refuge in the cold water at the mouth of Ashpole Creek.

MILE 135.2 (34.188992, -84.925236) Hardin Bridge. The last remaining operational iron-truss bridge on the Etowah River, it closed permanently in 2008. The new bridge just upstream was completed in 2011. The piers that still support the iron bridge predate the Civil War, and the former wooden bridge here was a key crossing point for troops during the Civil War. On river right, on both sides of the bridge, the remnants of trenches built for protection of the bridge remain. The trenches, however, didn't prevent the bridge from being burned during the Civil War. This is also an alternative launch site for this section. It is 6 miles from Hardin Bridge to U.S. 411, though the site does not offer a developed boat launch or parking area.

MILE 136.2 (34.177708, -84.935225) Stream Buffers & Riverfront Development. Riverfront development here serves as a reminder of the state's stream buffer laws. Georgia law prohibits the removal of vegetation and construction

FISH WEIR, ROCK GARDEN AREA, BARTOW COUNTY

HARDIN BRIDGE

activity within 25 feet of warm-water streams and within 50 feet of cold-water trout streams. Vegetated buffers along streams and rivers provide habitat for aquatic and terrestrial wildlife, help regulate stream temperatures, filter pollutants, and reduce stream-bank erosion.

MILE 137.6 (34.192400, -84.938422) Rock Garden. At this bend, the river spreads out into an impressive rock garden that requires you to pick your way carefully to find deep water. The rock garden also holds a fish weir that zigzags across the river, forming three distinct Vs. This has been a popular play spot since precolonial times. During the early spring, rock bluffs along the banks of the river here harbor beautiful shooting star wildflowers.

MILE 138.5 (34.192094, -84.953683) Fish Weir.

MILE 138.8 (34.194042, -84.955886) Island Ford. This island complex is the largest on the Etowah. Prior to the era of bridges, it was a popular ford. Today it is a popular camping spot for river travelers, but bear in mind that the islands are privately owned by several different parties. In the early spring, when drum in vast numbers congregate here to spawn, the water appears to boil as the fish thrash and splash in the shallow water. Two small ledges create a little excitement for paddlers about 300 yards downstream from the head of the island.

CRAYFISH ON ISLAND FORD, BARTOW COUNTY

MILE 139.6 (34.201083, -84.966453) Fish Weir.

MILE 140.9 (34.204136, -84.978328) Fish Weir.

MILE 141 (34.205767, -84.977650) Etowah Bend Gliderport. If you see gliders or ultralights touring above the river, this airstrip on river right is likely their origin. The small strip caters to those piloting experimental aircraft.

FISH WEIR NEAR ISLAND FORD,
BARTOW COUNTY

FISH WEIR, ROCK GARDEN AREA, BARTOW COUNTY

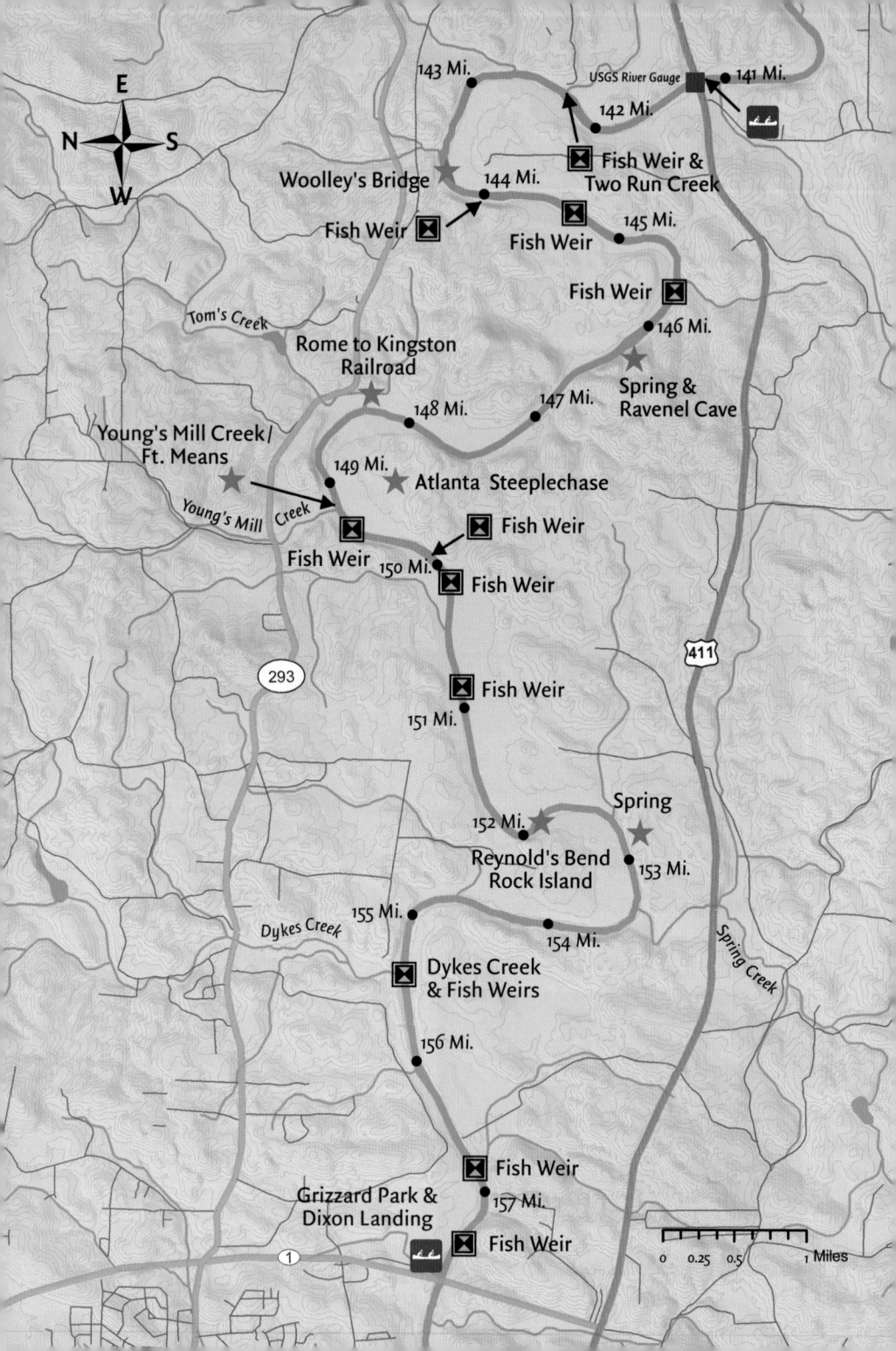

# Reynolds Bend

**Length** 16 miles (U.S. 411 to Ga. Loop 1 / Grizzard Park)

**Class** 1

**Time** 7–10 hours

**Minimum Level** The river here can be run year round. Releases from the Allatoona Dam can cause water levels to fluctuate dramatically. Paddlers should use caution when paddling this section during hydropower releases, which cause rapid rises in water levels. Release schedules are issued by the U.S. Army Corps of Engineers daily at midnight and can be retrieved by calling (706) 334-7213.

---

**River Gauge** The nearest river gauge is located at the U.S. 411 launch site: http://waterdata.usgs.gov/ga/nwis/uv?site_no=02395000.

**Launch Site** Currently, the best launch site is an undeveloped slope at the southeast corner of the U.S. 411 bridge. Most vehicles can access a road that leads to the top of this slope beneath the bridge. This is an extremely steep launch site. A ramp is planned for the southwest corner of the U.S. 411 bridge.

REYNOLDS BEND, FLOYD COUNTY

DIRECTIONS  The launch site can be accessed from U.S. 411 between Rome and Cartersville. Eastbound from Rome, cross the river and turn right onto the gravel road that parallels the highway here. Westbound from Cartersville, cross the river and make the first left, at Macedonia Road. Execute a U-turn, cross back over the river eastbound, and turn right onto the gravel road.

Take Out Site  Dixon Landing is a paved Department of Natural Resources boat ramp with large parking area located at the end of George Griffin Jr. Drive in the Rome-Floyd YMCA Sports Complex along Ga. Loop 1 on the outskirts of Rome.

DIRECTIONS  From the U.S. 411 launch site, travel west on U.S. 411 for 8.7 miles to Ga. Loop 1. Turn right on Ga. Loop 1 and proceed 1.9 miles to Turner Chapel Road. Turn right and then immediately right into the YMCA Sports Complex. Follow George Griffin Jr. Drive until it dead ends at Dixon Landing.

Description  From caves to springs to cliffs and shoals, this 16-mile section is varied, beautiful, and remote. Though some residential development encroaches, this remains the longest bridgeless section of the river. The paddle path crosses 12 Native American fish weirs and over the largest shoal on the river below Allatoona Dam.

Outfitters  Euharlee Creek Outfitters in Euharlee and the Coosa River Basin Initiative in Rome are the nearest canoe and kayak outfitters.

## Points of Interest

MILE 142.3 (34.221647, -84.981072) Fish Weir & Two Run Creek. Just upstream of the mouth of Two Run Creek is an excellent, intact fish dam, and along the creek adjacent to the river is the site of a sizable Cherokee Indian village that is shown on maps dating from as early as 1755. Many burials and artifacts have been discovered in the area. Upstream on Two Run Creek, Bartow County operates a wastewater treatment facility that discharges treated sewage into the creek.

MILE 143.6 (34.233644, -84.989358) Woolley's Bridge. All that remains of this pre–Civil War covered bridge are the rock piers. Union troops camped on the Andrew F. Woolley plantation here in May 1864—a key location because the bridge crossed the river where the Rome to Kingston Railroad paralleled it. Before the Union invasion, Woolley had employed the bridge to carry and sell lumber to the Confederate saltpeter operation at Ravenel Cave on the opposite side of the river (see below). Later in the war the bridge was burned, never to be rebuilt. Notice that these piers are not mortared, yet they remain even after more than 150 years.

MILE 144.1 (34.229150, -84.992103) Fish Weir.

MILE 144.6 (34.220894, -84.994233) Fish Weir.

MILE 145.6 (34.210869, -85.003264) Fish Weir.

MILE 146.3 (34.215772, -85.009644) Spring & Ravenel Cave. On river left on a high bank overlooking the shoals here is Ravenel Cave. This ancient cave was likely used as shelter by Native Americans, but it was most notably employed as a saltpeter mine during the Civil War. The Confederate Nitre Bureau mined caves throughout this area to extract nitrates to be used in the production of gunpowder. Proximity to water—an essential ingredient in the extraction process— is the likely reason this cave was mined. Soil was removed from the cave floor and through an arduous process that involved soaking the soil in water, adding wood ash and boiling off the water, potassium nitrate was created. The miners were known as peter monkeys and worked for low wages in the dark, damp caves. The workers at the Ravenel Cave were Confederate draftees who earned 60¢ per day. The Ravenel Cave was mined 1861–1862, but the nearby, and larger, Kingston Saltpeter Cave produced Confederate gunpowder until Sherman's invading troops destroyed the operation. According to a 1970 survey, the Ravenel Cave extends 203 feet into the bluff overlooking the river. The cave is located on private property. Directly opposite the cave, on river right, is a clear, cold spring run that is worth sticking your feet into.

ROCK ISLAND AT REYNOLDS BEND,
FLOYD COUNTY

MILE 148.3 (34.240942, -85.017019) Rome to Kingston Railroad. Paralleling the river on the north bank from Kingston to Rome is the now-abandoned Rome to Kingston Railroad. The line was originally chartered in 1839 as the Memphis Branch Railroad and Steamboat Co. of Georgia with a grand plan to connect Rome to Memphis, Tennessee (an idea for which local leaders still advocate— but as an interstate highway). It is considered the first rail line to attempt to connect steamboat traffic (on the Coosa at Rome) with the railroad. After the line was captured by Union troops, in July 1864 it helped avert a Union military disaster during the Allatoona Pass Battle as the line transported additional soldiers from Rome into the battle. The railroad also played a part in the famous Great Locomotive Chase during the Civil War. The Rome mail train picked up the Con-

FISH WEIR NEAR TOM'S CREEK, BARTOW COUNTY

federate's chase of the stolen "General" locomotive at Kingston. The railroad made its last run in October 1943. Trestles of the old railroad still remain over some Etowah tributaries, including this one at Tom's Creek, as well as near the mouth of Dykes Creek.

MILE 149.2 (34.244294, -85.029086) Young's Mill Creek / Ft. Means. Near the mouth of Young's Mill Creek in the spring of 1838, the U.S. military constructed Fort Means where nearby Cherokee Indians were gathered before their removal to the west. The fort served as the collection point for 467 Cherokee prisoners, one of whom was shot and killed for trying to escape. Captain John Means commanded 68 men from here. The accounts of the Cherokee Removal in the area differ depending upon who is telling the story. One account from the conquerors, goes like so: "After all the warning and with the soldiers in their midst, the inevitable day appointed found the Indians at work in their houses and in their fields. It is remembered as well as if it had been seen yesterday, that two or three dropped their hoes and ran as fast as they could when they saw the soldiers coming into the field. After that they made no effort to get out of the way. The men handled them gently, but picked them up in the road, in the field, anywhere they found them, part of a family at a time, and carried them to the post" (William Jasper Cotter, *My Autobiography* [1917], 39).

The account from a Cherokee named Oo-loo-cha, the widow of Sweet Water, went like so: "The soldiers came and took us from our home. They first surrounded our house and they took the mare while we were at work in the fields and they drove us out of doors and did not permit us to take anything with us, not even a second change of clothes. Only the clothes we had on. And they shut the doors after they turned us out. They would not permit any of us to enter the house to get any clothing, but drove us off to a fort that was built at New Echota (on the Oostanaula River near Calhoun). They kept us in the fort about three days and then marched us to Ross's Landing (Chattanooga). And still on foot, even our little children. They kept us for about three days at Ross's Landing and sent us off on a boat to this country" (qtd. in *Atlanta Journal-Constitution*, May 21, 2006).

FISH WEIR NEAR TOM'S CREEK, BARTOW COUNTY

MILE 149.2 (34.244294, -85.029086) Fish Weir. This weir is located just down-stream from the mouth of Young's Mill Creek

MILE 149.6 (34.241056, -85.032400) Atlanta Steeplechase. On river left here is the site of the Atlanta Steeplechase at Kingston Downs. An annual rite of Spring since 1966, the Steeplechase has been held at Kingston Downs since 1993. The horse race and high-style party attracts 25,000 people each year to this little bend of the Etowah and is considered Georgia largest single horse racing event. Proceeds from the event benefit various charities each year.

MILE 149.9 (34.234928, -85.034436) Fish Weir.

MILE 150.2 (34.232811, -85.037442) Fish Weir.

MILE 150.9 (34.231586, -85.050117) Fish Weir.

MILE 152.1 (34.224383, -85.066264) Reynold's Bend Rock Island. This rock is-land marks the beginning of a picturesque 2-mile loop in the river known as Reynold's Bend. The island is a great place to soak in the sun and go for a swim. Farther downriver are high rock bluffs on the south side of the river. The Bend is rich in history. Today, the property is still farmed as it has been for centuries. Had you been here in 1835, the residents included Cherokee Indians who went by

FISH WEIR AT TWO RUN CREEK, BARTOW COUNTY

Anglicized names like Pumpkinpile, Chicken Cook, Gone to Mill, Buffalo Fish, and Eagle on the Roost. After Pumpkinpile and his kind were forcibly removed from their homes, the Reynolds moved in, settling the "island" formed by the bend in 1847.

MILE 152.8 (34.215344, -85.067061) Spring. Along the base of the cliffs here, a cold, clear spring issues forth from a cleft in the rock at river left. During the summer it serves as a cold-water refuge for striped bass.

MILE 155.5 (34.237078, -85.083322) Dykes Creek & Fish Weirs. Visible near the mouth of Dykes Creek are the remains of a trestle of the Rome to Kingston Railroad. The 0.5 mile below Dykes Creek includes several indistinct Native American fish weirs.

MILE 156.8 (34.229725, -85.105825) Fish Weir. This is perhaps the most symmetrical fish weir along the length of the river, forming an almost perfect V.

MILE 157.5 (34.231147, -85.114667) Fish Weir.

MILE 157.6 (34.232283, -85.116231) Grizzard Park & Dixon Landing. This boat launch was completed in 2007 and named after the longtime Rome assistant city manager, Jim Dixon, who was instrumental in establishing this launch. At the time of its completion there was only one other public boat launch between Allatoona Dam and Rome.

NEAR REYNOLDS BEND, FLOYD COUNTY

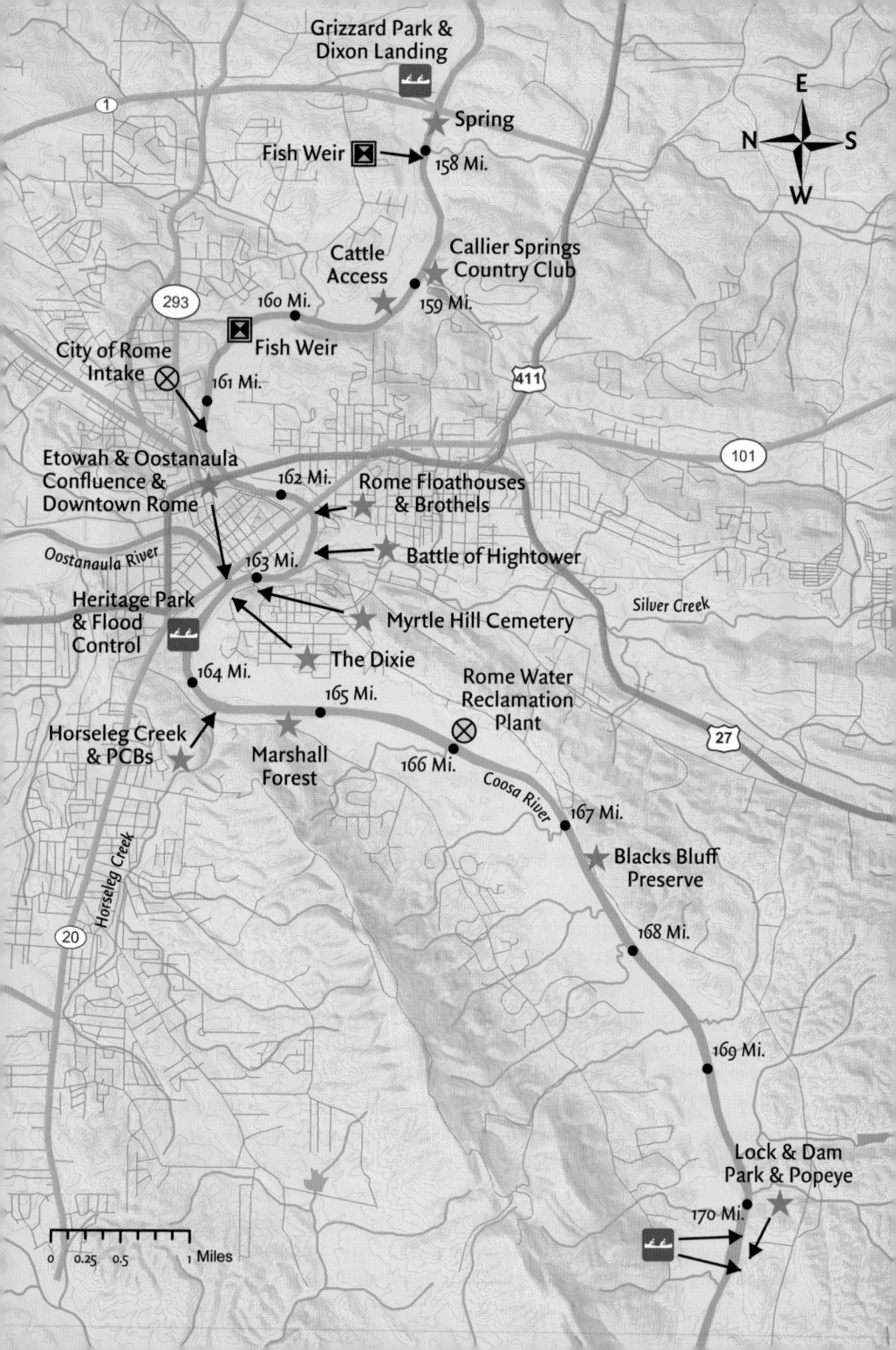

Grizzard Park &
Dixon Landing

Spring
158 Mi.

Fish Weir ⊠ →

Cattle
Access

Callier Springs
Country Club

293

160 Mi.

159 Mi.

City of Rome
Intake ⊗

⊠ Fish Weir

161 Mi.

411

101

Etowah & Oostanaula
Confluence &
Downtown Rome

162 Mi.

Rome Floathouses
& Brothels

Oostanaula River

163 Mi.

Battle of Hightower

Silver Creek

Heritage Park
& Flood
Control

Myrtle Hill Cemetery

The Dixie

Rome Water
Reclamation
Plant

164 Mi.

165 Mi.

27

Horseleg Creek
& PCBs

Marshall
Forest

⊗

166 Mi.

Coosa River

167 Mi.

20

Blacks Bluff
Preserve

168 Mi.

Horseleg Creek

169 Mi.

Lock & Dam
Park & Popeye

170 Mi.

0   0.25   0.5        1 Miles

E
N ✦ S
W

# Rome

**Length** 13 miles (Ga. Loop 1 / Grizzard Park to Lock and Dam Park)

**Class** I and optional Class II rapid at Lock and Dam Park

**Time** 5–7 hours

**Minimum Level** The river here can be run year round. Releases from the Allatoona Dam can cause water levels to fluctuate. Water released from the dam takes approximately 12 hours to reach Ga. Loop 1. Release schedules are issued by the U.S. Army Corps of Engineers daily at midnight and can be retrieved by calling (706) 334-7213.

---

**River Gauge** The nearest river gauge is located at the Ga. Loop 1 launch site: http://waterdata.usgs.gov/ga/nwis/uv?site_no=02395980.

**Launch Site** Dixon Landing is a paved Department of Natural Resources boat ramp with a large parking area located at the end of George Griffin Jr. Drive in the Rome-Floyd YMCA Sports Complex along Ga. Loop 1 on the outskirts of Rome.

DIRECTIONS The launch site can be accessed from U.S. 411 between Rome and Cartersville. Eastbound from Rome, turn left onto Ga. Loop 1 and travel for 1.9 miles. Turn right onto Turner Chapel Road and then immediately right again into the YMCA Sports Complex. Follow George Griffin Jr. Drive until it dead-ends at Dixon Landing.

**Take Out Site** Lock and Dam Park is a Floyd County park located on the Coosa River with overnight camping, showers, restroom facilities, picnic areas, walking trails, fishing areas, and camp store. Two take outs are available at the park. To avoid running the Class II rapid over the dam, take out upstream of the dam utilizing wooden steps and a canoe and kayak flume on river left. Otherwise, run the rapid and utilize the boat ramp on river left just below the lock. The park charges a nominal parking fee.

DIRECTIONS From U.S. 411 and Ga. Loop 1, proceed west toward Rome on U.S. 411. At the interchange in Rome, bear left onto U.S. 27 and U.S. 411 toward Cedartown and travel 3.4 miles. Turn right onto Walker Mountain Road and proceed 3.4 miles. Turn right at the entrance to Lock and Dam Park, and follow the road into park. The on-river journey from Grizzard Park to Lock and Dam Park is 13 miles.

**Alternative Take Out Site** An alternative, earlier take out site is located in Downtown Rome at Heritage Park on the Coosa just downstream from the confluence of the Etowah and Oostanaula Rivers. The on-river journey from Grizzard Park to Heritage Park is 6 miles.

DIRECTIONS From U.S. 411 and Ga. Loop 1, proceed west toward Rome on U.S. 411. At the interchange in Rome, bear right onto U.S. 27 and Ga. 20 toward Rome. Proceed 3.2 miles on Ga. 20 (Turner McCall Blvd.) to Martha Berry Blvd. / North 2nd Avenue. Turn left onto North 2nd Avenue and proceed 0.2 mile to the entrance to Heritage Park on the right.

Description A town-and-country tour, this 13-mile stretch of river travels from the rural outskirts of Rome into the heart of the city. In downtown Rome, the Etowah meets the Oostanaula River to form the Coosa River. Wide and deep, the Coosa winds westward through the city's suburbs, and down a historic steamboat path to Lock and Dam Park.

Outfitters The Coosa River Basin Initiative in Rome is the nearest canoe and kayak outfitters.

## Points of Interest

MILE 157.7 (34.233208, -85.120433) Spring. This unique spring carves a pocket from the riverbank, sending up a gusher of clear, cold water through sand and sediment. It is visible during low water on river left.

MILE 158.1 (34.234492, -85.124875) Fish Weir.

ROCK BLUFF ON ETOWAH, FLOYD COUNTY

MILE 158.9 (34.234333, -85.138964) Callier Springs Country Club. Fore! Watch for golf balls from river left in this stretch. Founded in 1939, Callier Springs boasts of willow trees around the course's water features that are said to be the offspring from a tree that grew on the original, St. Helena gravesite of Napoleon Bonaparte.

MILE 159.3 (34.237278, -85.143722) Cattle Access. Mooo! This site reveals the damage livestock can wreak on stream banks. While state agriculture agencies encourage cattle owners to exclude their animals from rivers and streams, no state laws mandate such practices. Livestock can denude riparian vegetation, creating erosion problems, and animal manure can contribute to elevated bacteria levels in the water.

MILE 160.3 (34.253289, -85.146056) Fish Weir.

MILE 161.2 (34.257050, -85.157878W) City of Rome Intake. On average, the City of Rome pumps a combined 6.2 million gallons a day from this location and its primary pumping station on the Oostanaula River. In recent years, the city has expressed interest in pumping all of its supply from the Etowah because it generally carries less sediment and other pollutants than the Oostanaula.

MILE 162.3 (34.245708, -85.167808) Rome Floathouses & Brothels. During the early 20th century, and especially during the Great Depression years of the late 1920s and 1930s, many of the destitute relied on rivers for their survival, taking up residences on shantyboats or floathouses where the living was cheap and where a trotline could always supply dinner. Rome had its share of these. At the 2nd Avenue Bridge, one notable floathouse operated as a brothel, an enterprise for which Rome became somewhat famous. About 1 mile upstream and just north of the river was another brothel, called Peggy's. A former textile mill worker, Peggy Snead operated what was considered a "clean house" and reportedly even paid city taxes on her business. City leaders looked the other way while the house operated quietly for several decades. An advertisement for the establishment even appeared in the 1963 Georgia Institute of Technology yearbook.

MILE 162.7 (34.246003, -85.173011) Battle of Hightower. On October 17, 1793, somewhere near the confluence of the Etowah and Oostanaula Rivers, a group of Creeks and Cherokees battled U.S. forces led by General John Sevier. Sevier and his men had pursued the Native peoples from Tennessee after an attack on white settlements there. In the brief Battle of Hightower, Sevier's troops forded the Etowah and met resistance from the American Indians led by the Cherokee chief, King Fisher. After he was killed in battle, King Fisher's force retreated east toward present-day Cartersville. A city recreational trail that parallels the river here is named in honor of King Fisher.

MILE 163.1 (34.252478, -85.176817) Myrtle Hill Cemetery. Rising above the South Broad Bridge in downtown Rome, Myrtle Hill and the cemetery on its flanks is the final resting place of 20,000 people, including 370 Confederate and Union

WINTER ON ETOWAH RIVER IN ROME, FLOYD COUNTY

soldiers of the Civil War; Ellen Axson Wilson, the wife of President Woodrow Wilson (Wilson courted Miss Axson in her hometown); and the great-grandparents of rock 'n' roll legend Jim Morrison. Morrison's forebears came to Rome around 1886 and operated the Morrison-Trammel Brick Company. A four-year-old Jim attended his great-grandmother's funeral at the cemetery in 1947. Early Romans chose this spot for a cemetery because it was above the reach of the river's frequent floods.

MILE 163.2 (34.253831, -85.176989) Etowah & Oostanaula Confluence & Downtown Rome. Where the Etowah and Oostanaula meet to form the Coosa is the heart of Rome, founded in 1834. Rome was a thriving river town during the 1800s and early 1900s. The 100 block of Broad Street is known as the Cotton Block because this is where cotton was loaded onto steamboats bound downriver. In 1873, six steamboats operated out of Rome. Between Rome and Gadsden, Alabama, there were some 140 landings. When flowing within their banks and carrying cotton, the rivers were a blessing, but periodic freshets were a curse. Rome's most famous flood occurred in 1886, when parts of the downtown were under more than 10 feet of water. During high water, the paddle wheeler *Mitchell* steamed up Broad Street, took a left on Fourth Avenue and crossed the Oostanaula in an effort to save a horse. Thirty homes were washed downstream, along with three bridges, prompting the city to raise the level of Broad Street by 8 feet. What are now recognized as the first floors of many historic downtown buildings are actually the original second floors. The iron railroad bridge over the Oostanaula at the confluence was designed as a pivot bridge, allowing the span to swing parallel to the river from its center footing, permitting the passage of river steamers. At the confluence, the two rivers have disparate water temperatures, especially notable during the summer. The Etowah runs noticeably cooler because of releases of cold water from the base of Allatoona Dam—a change in river habitat that has, in part, caused the demise of many fish and mussel species in the Etowah.

MILE 163.3 (34.253969, -85.177958) The Dixie. Lying along the banks of the Etowah and Coosa Rivers are the remains of the paddle wheeler *Dixie*. The wood structure of the boat is discernible in low water, along with cribbing from the wharf where she once docked. While moored at a landing in 1914, the boat burned and sank, reportedly after a galley fire.

MILE 163.4 (34.255039, -85.178811) Heritage Park & Flood Control. A boat ramp at the city's Heritage Park provides a take out location and views of Rome's extensive levee system. Completed in 1939 by the U.S. Army Corps of Engineers, the levee saved portions of the city from the freshets but proved ineffective at preventing floods in the downtown business district. The construction of Allatoona Dam in the late 1940s finally remedied that problem.

ROPE SWING IN DOWNTOWN ROME, FLOYD COUNTY

MILE 164.3 (34.255483, -85.191897) Horseleg Creek & PCBs. This creek, which drains much of West Rome, has been impacted by PCB contamination from the General Electric Medium Transformer Plant in Rome. A known carcinogen, PCBs left the GE facility in stormwater that emptied into Horseleg and other creeks. GE, under order from Georgia's Environmental Protection Division (EPD), has done extensive excavation along Horseleg to remove contaminants. During the years that PCBs were used at the plant, an unknown number of GE employees used PCBs at their homes as a termite deterrent, dust suppressant, and wood treatment. And, an undetermined number of residents used PCB-contaminated sludge

RAPID AT LOCK AND DAM, FLOYD COUNTY

from Rome's wastewater treatment plant as fertilizer for gardens and farms. Today, the extent of PCB contamination in the area is still not fully known, and PCBs continue to be found in fishes of the Coosa River basin, resulting in fish consumption advisories for most rivers and streams in the area. The cleanup of PCBs at the GE facility and in and around Rome is expected to take decades.

MILE 164.7 (34.247703, -85.192650) Marshall Forest. Located on river right here, Marshall Forest is a 300-acre Nature Conservancy preserve that is home to one of the last remaining stands of old-growth forest in the Ridge and Valley Province, a geographical corridor that runs from Pennsylvania to Alabama. More than 300 species of plants, including 55 tree species can be found in the forest. Designated Georgia's first National Natural Landmark in 1966, the forest is said to be the country's only old-growth forest located within a city limits.

MILE 166.1 (34.229653, -85.197114) Rome Water Reclamation Plant. Until 1965, when this facility was constructed, the City of Rome had limited sewage treatment. It's said that Coosa River anglers of the 1950s routinely reeled in toilet paper on their lines. Beginning in 2001, the city, under order of the EPD, embarked on a $38 million upgrade to the plant, which was completed in 2008. The facility can now treat up to 36 million gallons a day of sewage.

MILE 167.3 (34.217064, -85.209631) Blacks Bluff Preserve. The bluffs—500-million-year-old Conasauga limestone—are visible on river left rising above Black's Bluff Road, which runs parallel to the Coosa. The Nature Conservancy has protected 132 acres along the river here because of its botanical diversity. A massive natural rock garden, the north-facing slope of the bluffs keeps things cool and moist, and the alkalinity of the lime-rich soil provide habitat for endangered large-flowered skullcap and the state-endangered limerock arrowwood. The site includes limestone caves that are home to cave salamanders.

MILE 170.4 (34.200411, -85.257078) Lock & Dam Park & Popeye. In the 1800s, this was the site of a troublesome shoals known as Horseleg Shoals, which made navigation difficult for the paddle wheelers. The solution was to build a small dam and a lock to move the ships and the cotton they carried up and down the river. The lock and dam operated from 1913 until 1941. Its most lasting contribution to the Coosa Valley and the world is as the birthplace of the cartoon character Popeye. Popeye's creator, Tom Sims, was the son of a boat captain who operated ships on the Coosa River for the U.S. Army Corps of Engineers, including one called the *Leota*. The stories of Popeye are drawn from Sims's childhood on the Coosa. Sims said, "Fantastic as Popeye is, the whole story is based on facts. As a boy I was raised on the Coosa River. When I began writing the script for Popeye I put my characters back on the old *Leota* that I knew as a boy, transformed it into a ship and made the Coosa River a salty sea" (*Rome News-Tribune*, Feb. 11, 1979).

# Animals and Plants along Georgia Rivers

Species are arranged, as best as possible, into groups similar to one another. Mammals move from aquatic toward terrestrial; birds from water birds to birds of prey and wild turkey; fish from cold-water to warm-water species; reptiles and amphibians from smallest (frogs) to largest (alligators), with snakes and turtles grouped together; and plants from largest to smallest, with large trees first, then smaller flowering trees, shrubs, understory vegetation (ferns, canes, wildflowers), and finally aquatic vegetation.

## Mammals

### Beaver (*Castor canadensis*)

Reaching lengths of up to 4 feet (including the iconic paddle-shaped tail) and weights of up to 60 pounds, beavers are North America's largest rodents. On Georgia rivers they usually live in burrows in the banks, rather than in constructed dens. They are rarely seen during daylight hours, but along the shore, "bleached" sticks that they have stripped of bark are a sign of beaver activity. Beavers are keystone species for clean water, as the wetlands they construct serve as natural filters that capture sediment and other pollutants and provide habitat for many other species.

### Muskrat (*Ondatra zibethica*)

This common aquatic rodent grows to lengths of 2 feet (including its foot-long, hairless tail). Though primarily nocturnal, muskrats can sometimes be seen foraging for food during the day. Its riverbank dens are concealed via an underwater entrance. Among its more notable attributes: lips that close behind its teeth to allow underwater feeding, and a prodigious reproductive cycle. They commonly bear four litters of five to seven young each year. They eat primarily plants but also consume mussels, frogs, and crayfish. If you come across a pile of small mussels, it's likely the site of a muskrat feast.

## Otter (*Lutra Canadensis*)

Reaching lengths of over 4 feet (including its long fur-covered tail), river otters are long and slender compared to muskrats and beavers. They commonly comman-deer abandoned muskrat or beaver dens for their homes, but unlike their aquatic neighbors they are carnivores, using their swimming skills to capture fish, crayfish, frogs, salamanders, snakes, and turtles. They also partake of mussels and even

birds. Although they are rarely seen during the day, you sometimes hear their barks and squeals and see them in the early morning or at twilight.

## Groundhog (*Marmota monax*)

Often mistaken for an otter or beaver, groundhogs (also known as woodchucks) frequent areas where woodlands meet open spaces—like along rivers—where they forage on grasses, plants, fruits, and even tree bark. Yes, woodchucks do chuck wood. Though they are not aquatic, they do swim . . . and climb trees, but den in the ground, lending them their common name. Groundhogs grow to about 2 feet in length and have a short (7–9 inches) furry tail.

## Raccoon (*Procyon lotor*)

Known for its black mask and black-ringed tail, rac-coons are riverside foragers. While they are highly adaptive and opportunistic, they prefer habitats near water (for food) that are filled with mature hard-woods (for shelter). The Latin *lotor* means washer—a reference to the raccoon's penchant for washing its food before eating. Theories abound about this practice, but to date scientists have not reached any conclusions. Raccoons feed on crayfish, fiddler crabs, fish, and even some snakes as well as fruits and acorns. They grow to lengths of 3 feet and can weigh as much as 20 pounds.

## Opossum
### (Didelphis virginian)

About the size of your average house cat, opossums
are North America's only
marsupial. After birth (following a gestation period
of just 12 days), infants
crawl into a pouch on their
mother's abdomen, where
they are suckled for about 70 days. They are unique for additional reasons . . . they
have more teeth (50) than any other land mammal in the world, and they are im-
mune to snake venom and kill and eat venomous snakes.

## Coyote (Canis latrans)

A nonnative species to Georgia, coyotes have
filled the ecosystem niche vacated by the red
wolf, which is a critically endangered species.
In the late 1960s, coyotes were reported in only
23 Georgia counties, but in 2010 they could be
found in all 159 counties. Their success in the
state is attributable to their adaptability: they'll
eat anything and live anywhere.

## Armadillo (Dasypus novemcinctus)

Originally restricted to Texas, nine-banded armadillos have pushed steadily east
during the past century and are now found throughout Georgia except in the far
north. Their preferred habitat is along streams, and they cross water either by
swimming or by walking on the stream bottom while holding their breath. Their
primary food is insects,
which they forage from
the ground, employing a
sensitive nose, a sticking
tongue, and feet adapted
for digging.

## Gray Squirrel (*Sciurus carolinensis*)

The most commonly seen native mammal in Georgia, adaptable gray squirrels survive in many habitats but prefer hardwood forests, where nuts and acorns provide the bulk of their pound-a-week dietary requirements. Cracking the forest masts requires specialized equipment—namely incisor teeth that are continuously ground down but also continuously grow—up to 6 inches per year. Fossil records show that the gray squirrel roamed North America 50 million years ago.

## White-tail Deer (*Odocoileus virginianus*)

A species nearly lost to Georgia, white-tailed deer survive now because of restocking and wildlife management programs initiated during the mid-20th century. In 2002, Georgia's Department of Natural Resources estimated the state's deer population at 1.2 million. Hunting season in Georgia for white-tail deer runs from September to January, depending on the area.

## Black Bear (*Ursus americanus*)

Prior to the 19th century, black bears were abundant in Georgia, but habitat loss and overhunting dramatically reduced their population. Restrictions on hunting and other management practices implemented during the 20th century have allowed the species to recover. Georgia's Department of Natural Resources estimates a population of more than 5,000. Their range is mostly restricted to the North Georgia mountains, the bottomland forests along the Ocmulgee River, and the Okefenokee Swamp. Reaching weights of up to 500 pounds, black bears are the state's heftiest land mammals, but their weight doesn't slow them down. They are excellent climbers, swim well, and can run at speeds up to 30 miles per hour.

## Red Fox (*Vulpes vulpes*) and Gray Fox (*Urocyon cinereoargenteus*)

The gray fox is Georgia's only remaining native member of the canine family, but along Georgia rivers you're more likely to encounter the red fox, a species introduced from Europe by early settlers. That's because the red fox is more common along forest edges, fields, and river bottoms, whereas the gray stays primarily in wooded areas. Grays are distinguished by a mottled gray coat, a black-tipped tail, and the unique ability (for canines) to climb trees. Reds have a rust-colored coat and a white-tipped tail.

## Birds

### Kingfisher (*Megaceryle alcyon*)

A slate-blue back, wings, and breast belt along with a white belly and crested head distinguish this patroller of riverbanks. Feeding mostly on fish, the kingfisher spends its time perched in trees over the water. In the spring, they construct nest burrows in riverbanks, and mating pairs produce five to eight offspring. Kingfishers, which have a distinctive cry (a loud, harsh rattle usually delivered in flight) are among the most common birds sighted along Georgia rivers.

### Great Blue Heron (*Ardea herodias*)

The largest North American heron, great blues grow to almost 4 feet in length and have a 6-foot wingspan. Silent sentinels along riverbanks, they wade slowly but strike with their bill with lighting quickness, feeding mostly on fish, frogs,

and crustaceans, which they swallow whole. Herons engage in elaborate courtship displays and nest in colonies located high up in trees along rivers and lakes. When disturbed, they sometimes let out a loud, distinctive squawk as they flee.

## Green Heron (*Butorides virescens*)

A small, stocky wading bird reaching lengths of 18 inches, the Green Heron is one of the few tool-using birds. It commonly drops bait onto the surface of the water and grabs the small fish that are attracted. It uses a variety of baits and lures, including crusts of bread, insects, earthworms, twigs, or feathers. It feeds on small fish, invertebrates, insects, frogs, and other small animals.

## Great Egret (*Ardea alba*)

Like the Great Blue Heron, this large wading bird reaches lengths of close to 4 feet, but it is distinguished by its all-white plumage and black legs and feet. It is more commonly seen along the Georgia coast. It has the distinction of being the symbol of the National Audubon Society because when the society was founded in 1905, the egrets were being hunted into extinction for their plumes, which were used to decorate hats and clothing.

## Osprey (*Pandion haliaetus*)

Known as fish hawks because they feed almost exclusively on live fish, ospreys glide above open water and then dive-bomb their prey, sometimes completely submerging themselves to secure their quarry. Studies have shown that ospreys catch fish on at least 25 percent of their dives, with some kill rates as high as 70 percent. The average time they spend hunting before making a catch is about 12 minutes. Ospreys have a wingspan of 4–6 feet and can be con-

fused with bald eagles because of their white head and brown wings. In flight, however, the white underside of their wings gives them away as eagle imposters. They build large nests of sticks in trees and artificial platforms high above open water.

## Bald Eagle
### (*Haliaeetus leucocephalus*)

The bald eagle has been emblazoned on the Great Seal of the United States since 1782 and has been a spiritual symbol for Native people far longer than that. Once endangered by hunting and pesticides, bald eagles have flourished under federal protection. Though regal-looking birds, their behavior is often less than noble. While they do hunt and capture live prey, they more often obtain their food by harassing and stealing it from other birds (like the osprey) or by dining on carrion. They can be found on rivers throughout Georgia.

## Turkey Vulture (*Cathartes aura*)

This large, black bird with a bald, red head can often be seen along Georgia rivers feeding on carrion that has washed onto sandbars or become stranded on strainers. Turkey vultures soar to great heights searching for food, and unique among birds, they have a strong sense of smell, which helps them locate it. They have a wing span of 4–6 feet and are easily identified in flight by their two-toned wings—silvery to light gray flight feathers with black wing linings.

## Wild Turkey (*Meleagris gallopavo*)

Wild turkeys were almost hunted to extinction by the 20th century, but conservation efforts implemented after the 1930s have resulted in a dramatic increase in populations. Benjamin Franklin lobbied for the wild turkey to be featured in the national emblem instead of the bald eagle. He thought the turkey a more noble and beautiful bird than the thieving, carrion-eating bald eagle. Turkeys feed on nuts, seeds, fruits, insects, and salamanders and are commonly seen in floodplain forests along the river. And, they do fly . . . on wingspans of more than 4 feet.

# Fish

### Brook Trout (*Salvelinus fontinalis*)

The East Coast's only native trout species, brookies require cold, clear water to survive and as such are found only in the highest headwaters of the North Georgia mountains. Aquatic insects, like mayflies, caddisflies, and stoneflies as well as fish and crayfish make up the bulk of their diet. There are 5,400 miles of trout streams in Georgia. Nonnative rainbow and brown trout can be found in all those streams, but only 142 miles support native brook trout.

## Longnose Gar (*Lepisosteus osseus*)

This prehistoric fish is known for its long, cylindrical body and pointed snout filled with many sharp teeth. Little changed since the day of the dinosaur, its body is armored in thick hard scales that Native Americans employed as arrowheads. Its evolutionary longevity might be attributed to its unique ability to acquire oxygen from air. During summer months, when oxygen levels in water decrease, it can often be spotted just beneath the surface and surfacing to "gulp" air—a trait that makes it well adapted for surviving in warm, shallow water.

## Striped Bass (*Morone saxatilis*)

Easily identified by rows of dark horizontal lines on their flanks, striped bass are one of Georgia's native anadromous fishes, meaning they move from saltwater to freshwater to spawn. Female stripers can carry as many as 4 million eggs. Once fertilized by males, the eggs need at least 50 miles of free-flowing river to hatch. Less than 1 percent survive to adulthood. Dams have interrupted most migratory routes along the Atlantic and Gulf coasts, but stocking programs maintain populations on inland lakes and rivers.

## Channel Catfish (*Ictalurus punctatus*)

One of 20 catfish species found in Georgia, channel cats are the most commercially important catfish species in North America and are commonly raised in large aquaculture operations.

In the wild they are nighttime hunters, feeding on everything from small fish to algae and insects. They aren't fazed by low-visibility situations thanks to their distinctive whiskers and skin being covered in "taste buds." These external sensors help them locate food by taste rather than sight.

## Reptiles and Amphibians

### Green Tree Frog (*Hyla cinerea*)

Georgia's official state amphibian, the green tree frog primarily resides along South Georgia rivers. A green back, a white belly, and a white, yellow, or iridescent stripe down each flank distinguish this frog among the state's 30 native species. Protecting riparian vegetation along water bodies helps ensure the survival of this and other frogs.

### Snapping Turtle (*Chelydra serpentine*)

Snapping turtles are not commonly seen on Georgia rivers because they rarely bask. Instead, they spend much of their lives on the river bottom under cover of vegetation and mud, where they feed on aquatic vegetation and ambush fish, crayfish, frogs, and anything else that happens to cross their paths. They are most often spotted from May to June, when females leave the water to lay eggs in nearby sandbars or loamy soil. Young hatch out from August through October.

### River Cooter (*Pseudemys concinna*)

The consummate baskers of Georgia rivers, you may often spot river cooters sunning themselves on logs or rocks. At the first sign of danger, they plunge into the water, often creating loud splashes. They grow to 12 inches in length, feed mostly on aquatic vegetation and algae, and lay their eggs in sandbars along riverbanks. A pile of broken white shells on a sandbar in August and September is a likely indication of a cooter nest. Georgia limits the wild harvest of river cooters and other turtles that have come under increasing pressure due to demand in Asian food markets.

## Spiny Softshell Turtle
### (*Apalone Spinifera*)

Sometimes described as a pancake with legs, the spiny softshell turtle sports a flat leathery shell. Males and young have dark spots on the shell that are absent in females, which can grow to lengths of 17 inches (males top out at 9 inches). Unique in the turtle world, soft shells have the ability to obtain oxygen from adaptations on their throats and anuses, enabling them to remain submerged for up to 5 hours. They are carnivorous, ambushing unsuspecting prey while lying partially covered on the river bottom.

## Banded Watersnake (*Nerodia fasciata*)

The most common snake of Georgia's Coastal Plain rivers, streams, lakes, and wetlands, banded water snakes are often spotted basking on rocks, logs, and limbs overhanging the water's edge. They vary in color from light brown or reddish to black in ground-color with darker crossbands, and hunt for fish and amphibians in shallow water. A similar species, the northern watersnake (*Nerodia sipedon*) is restricted to North Georgia.

## Water Moccasin
### (*Agkistrodon piscivorous*)

Georgia is home to 11 species of water snakes; only the water moccasin is venomous. Unfortunately, five species of water snakes are similar in appearance to water moccasins, making positive identification of moccasins tricky. Moccasins are best differentiated from other snakes by their behavior and habitat preference. They are restricted to Georgia's Coastal

Plain and southern portions of the Piedmont. In these regions, they bask on land, stumps, or logs near the water's surface and prefer slow-moving streams, swamps, and backwaters. Common water snakes, on the other hand, bask on limbs and shrubs overhanging the water and prefer large, open reservoirs and rivers. Finally, swimming moccasins hold their heads above the water and their bodies ride on the surface of the water; water snakes swim below the surface. It is illegal to kill nonvenomous snakes in Georgia.

### Alligator (*Alligator mississippiensis*)

The largest predator in the state, alligators can grow to 16 feet in length and weigh as much as 800 pounds. They are found only in South Georgia, below the fall line running from Columbus to Augusta. Once a federally protected species, alligator populations have rebounded, and they are now common within their range. During warm weather, they can be spotted basking along riverbanks or patrolling the water with only their snouts visible above the water's surface. Since 1980, there have been only nine confirmed alligator attacks on humans in Georgia, only one of which was fatal.

## Macroinvertebrates

This group of animals includes mollusks (mussels and snails), arthropods (crayfish and sowbugs), and aquatic insects (mayflies, stoneflies, etc.). Though usually small, they form the base of the aquatic food chain and play critical roles in clean water. Their life cycles and adaptations are among the most interesting in nature, and their presence, or lack thereof, can be an indicator of the health of a water body.

## Native Freshwater Snails

Georgia is home to 67 species of freshwater snails that range in size from 0.1 inch to more than 1 inch in length. Easily overlooked because they dwell on the river bottom, they play an important role in river ecosystems. They scour rocks and other debris of algae, helping maintain healthy water and providing suitable habitat for aquatic insects. Snails, in turn, are an important food source for other wildlife.

## Native Freshwater Mussels

Historically, Georgia was home to 126 species of freshwater mussels. However, many have become extinct due to habitat changes wrought by the construction of dams and water pollution. The state is currently home to 14 federally protected species. Because they are filter feeders, meaning they remove nutrients from the water, they play a critical role in clean rivers. They come in various colors, shapes, and sizes, with some species growing to the size of dinner plates. Because their unique life cycle involves fish carrying young mussels on their gills, the loss of some fish species has contributed to declining mussel populations.

## Asian Clams
### (*Corbicula fluminea*)

This nonnative, invasive clam is the most commonly seen mollusk in Georgia rivers. Corbicula entered the United States in the Pacific Northwest and are now found in 38 states. Prolific reproducers and adaptable to many habitats, corbicula have flourished where native mussels have struggled. In doing so they have filled a food void. Numerous species of fish as well as crayfish, raccoons, muskrats, and otters feed on them. They are distinguished from native mussels by their size, rarely growing to more than 1 inch in length.

## Crayfish

Georgia is home to 73 species of crayfish, many of which are restricted to isolated populations in specific regions of the state. On Georgia rivers, you'll find them beneath rocks and debris on the river bottom, though some species create extensive burrows in the soil near wetlands areas. They are protected by a hard exoskeleton that, as adults, they outgrow and molt once or twice each year. In combination with diminishing stream health because of pollution, the introduction of nonnative crayfish used as bait by anglers poses a serious threat to Georgia's native crayfish.

## Hellgrammite (Dobsonfly Larvae)

Flip over a rock in a healthy to moderately healthy stream in Georgia, and you'll find these frightening-looking creatures that are distinguished by two large mandibles. Reaching up to 3 inches in length, the hellgrammite is a predator of other aquatic insects and is a favorite food of popular game fish species. Dobsonfly larvae develop for one to three years in the water, crawl from the water, dig a cavity to pupate, and emerge 14–28 days later as adults. The adults survive just long enough to mate and lay eggs. The females deposit their eggs, encased in a white covering, on overhanging leaves, logs, tree trunks, or rocks so that when the larvae hatch they fall into the water.

## Dragonfly Nymphs

While adult dragonflies are always associated with water, by far most of a dragonfly's life is spent in the water, not hovering above it. Dragonfly nymphs live in the water for up to four years before crawling out for their final molts and becoming adults. The skin (exuvia) left on rocks

and plants along the water can be found long after the molt has occurred. Adult dragonflies generally survive less than two months. Dragonflies are appreciated for their efforts in mosquito control. Nymphs eat mosquito larvae from the water, while adults can consume hundreds of flying mosquitos daily, earning them the moniker "mosquito hawks."

## Mayfly Nymphs

Because all mayfly nymphs in an area commonly transform to adults at the same time, mayflies are known for their massive swarms that occur during the summer months. Their life underwater in Georgia rivers consists of clinging to the underside of rocks, where they feed mostly on algae. After a prolonged period (in some cases more than two years), they crawl out of the water to transform into adults. Nymphs are easily identified by their three hairlike tails (though sometimes only two). With fossil evidence confirming their existence more than 300 million years ago, they are believed to be the oldest living winged insects.

# Trees and Plants
## Sycamore (*Platanus occidentalis*)

A dominant deciduous tree of river corridors, sycamores are easily identified by their dark-brown to gray bark that peels and flakes, revealing a white inner bark. Sycamores also sport large, multilobed leaves that turn yellow and then tan in the fall, as well as conspicuous fruits—a round woody ball that in the winter breaks into many soft, fluffy seeds. Native Americans fashioned the large trunks of sycamores into dugout canoes; beaver, squirrel, and muskrat eat the fruits; juncos and finches eat the seeds. They grow to 80–100 feet tall with a spread of 40–50 feet.

## River Birch (*Betula nigra*)

The deciduous river birch is know for its reddish brown to cinnamon-red bark that peels back in tough papery layers, giving the trunk a ragged appearance. In the winter, its fruits and flowers are conspicuous. Male flowers, dangling woody tubes (catkins) that are 1–3 inches long, can be seen on the ends of stems, along with the remnants of the previous year's fruit—1-inch woody cones. In the spring, the male flowers release pollen, fertilizing the emerging female flowers that produce the fruit. Growing to heights of 80 feet, birch play an important role in stabilizing stream banks with their extensive root system. Extracts from the tree are used in herbal treatments for gout, rheumatism, and kidney stones.

## Black Willow (*Salix nigra*)

The deciduous black willow is a dominant tree of Georgia's Coastal Plain rivers, especially along sandbars. Distinguished by its long, lance-like leaves, willows are perhaps most conspicuous in the midsummer, when their cottony seeds are born on the wind, falling to the river and sometimes forming large floating mats of white fluff. Their fibrous roots play a critical role in stabilizing stream banks, and a compound derived from their bark is known for its fever-reducing and pain-killing effects. A synthetically produced variety is found in modern aspirin. Willows can attain heights of up to 60 feet.

## Black Walnut (*Juglans nigra*)

Because it thrives in full sunlight, the black walnut is often found in the open, well-lit spaces afforded by riverbanks. In the fall, after dropping its leaves it then drops its golf-ball-sized fruits, and it is not uncommon to find them floating down the river. After removing their husk (which stain hands and clothes), the hard, brown corrugated nut can—with considerable work—be broken to obtain the meat. Walnuts are high in antioxidants and beneficial fats and have more protein than any other nut—thus they are prized by squirrel, deer, and people. Walnuts typically grow to 60–70 feet, but specimens over 100 feet are common.

## Red Maple (*Acer rubrum*)

Aptly named because its buds, winged seeds, leaf stems, and leaves (in the fall) are all brilliant red, the red maple is one of the earliest flowering trees of the spring. Its buds sprout long before vegetation appears, and once pollinated, these buds mature to bright red, winged seeds that twirl off, helicopter-like, in the wind. Red maples also change color in the fall long before other trees have begun their transformation. Because of its tolerance for moist soils, it is commonly referred to as swamp maple.

## Water Oak (*Quercus nigra*)

A dominant oak of bottomland forests and riparian buffers, water oak sport leaves that resemble a small kitchen spatula—narrow at the base and widening at a lobed end. Though deciduous, young water oaks are known to hold their leaves through the winter, while leaves on older specimens persist well into the winter. The tree's acorns are important food for squirrel, deer, and wild turkey. They commonly grow to a height of 50–80 feet.

## American Hornbeam (*Carpinus caroliniana*)

A tree of the bottomland forest understory, hornbeams grow to 20–30 feet in height and thrive in the shade beneath larger trees. Leaves are egg-shaped with distinct veins radiating from the mainstem, ending in toothed leaf edges. The tree's fruit is conspicuous, as the nutlets are contained within a three-winged, narrow, leaflike bract. The leaves turn yellow, orange, and red in the fall and sometimes persist on the tree into the winter, causing confusion with the beech tree, which also holds its leaves in the winter.

## Tag Alder (*Alnus serrulata*)

Fibrous roots and flexible stems make this a favorite species for stream bank restoration projects. A shrub-like tree, it grows to heights of 8–12 feet and tends to form thickets along rivers and streams. Like river birch, during the winter months it is easily identified by the presence of last year's fruit (0.5-inch woody cones) and dangling catkins, which though brown in the winter bloom bright yellow in the early spring. The bark and leaves of the alder have historically been used as an astringent to treat internal bleeding as well as external wounds.

## Catalpa (*Catalpa bignonioides*)

Perhaps the showiest bloomer of Georgia's river corridors, the catalpa produces large clusters of white bell-shaped blossoms with purple spots and two large orange markings at the throat. In the summer, these fertilized blooms produce long (up to 16 inches) bean-like pods that hang beneath the tree's heart-shaped leaves. The pods ripen and turn brown in the fall, eventually splitting to release paper-thin fringed seeds that float off in a breeze. Catalpas are best known as the sole host for catalpa sphinx moth larvae—a black-and-yellow, horned caterpillar highly prized by anglers as fish bait.

## Mountain Laurel (*Kalmia latifolia*)

A showy shrub of the Georgia mountains and Piedmont (and occasionally the Coastal Plain), mountain
laurel produces abundant clusters of white-to-pink
honeycomb-shaped blooms in the early spring. It
is commonly seen along Georgia rivers at rocky
outcroppings. Its evergreen leaves are conspicuous in
the winter, but can be confused with rhododendron,
another evergreen, flowering shrub. Rhododendron
leaves are larger and more elongated. The leaves of
the mountain laurel, as well as those of rhododendron
and azalea, are toxic if consumed in quantity.

## Piedmont Azalea (*Rhododendron canescens*)

In 1979, the Georgia General Assembly designated
wild azaleas as the state wildflower, and with good
reason: Georgia is home to 10 of North America's
16 native azalea species. Almost all are partial to
moist woodlands and stream banks, thus traveling
Georgia's rivers you are likely to encounter many,
from the hammock sweet azalea on the coast to the
sweet azalea of the mountains. Piedmont azalea is
among the most common. Its pink-to-white flowers
appear from March through early May and emit a
sweet, musky fragrance. Azaleas are considered
shrubs and rarely grow taller than 15 feet.

## Dogwood (*Cornus florida*)

Perhaps the best known of North America's native flowering trees, dogwoods are common understory trees in floodplain forests along Georgia's rivers. The iconic four-petal, white flower blooms from March through April. In the fall the leaves turn scarlet red and the red berries become very conspicuous. Songbirds, wild turkeys, and a host of mammals—from chipmunks to bears—feed on these berries. Historically, humans have employed the root bark as an antidiarrheal agent, fever reducer, and pain reliever. Dogwoods grow up to 20 feet in height with a spread of up to 30 feet.

## Persimmon (*Diospyros virginiana*)

A lover of bottomland forests, persimmons can be found growing along streams and rivers in Georgia, and occasionally the prized fruit can be plucked from branches overhanging the water in the late fall. The plum-sized pulpy fruit filled with large seeds is very sweet, but only after it is fully ripe (usually after a hard frost). Unless the fruits are fully orange to black—and soft—avoid them. Unripe persimmons can leave you puckering and longing for a drink of water. Birds, deer, and hogs eat the fruits and thus help distribute the seeds throughout the forest. Persimmons can grow to 80 feet in height.

## Dog Hobble (*Leucothoe fontanesiana*)

Like its close relatives rhododendron and mountain laurel, this member of the heath family is an evergreen shrub, making it easy to identify during the winter. In the spring, it produces showy clusters of small, white bell-shaped blossoms that are often concealed beneath the leaves. Its common name is derived from its dense tangle of arching branches that make traveling through it a chore. Hunters say that bears run through stands of dog hobble to distance themselves from pursuing hounds. The leaves and flower nectar are poisonous to both humans and animals.

## Yellowroot (*Xanthorhiza simplicissima*)

A streamside dweller throughout the state, this unique shrub derives its common name from the color of its roots and inner bark. In the early spring before its leaves appear, it puts out 2-to-4-inch clusters of purple star-shaped flowers. The leaves are unique; their deeply toothed edges giving them a lacey appearance. In the fall they turn yellow, bronze, or red. It has long been recognized for its medicinal properties in treating ulcers of the mouth and stomach. In tends to grow in dense thickets and reaches no more than 3 feet in height.

## Elderberry (*Sambucus nigra*)

Common along streams, springs, and swamps, the elderberry is a favorite of songbirds and humans thanks to its abundant purple berries that appear in the late summer and early fall. More than 50 birds are known to feed on elderberries, and humans transform the berries into wines, jellies, and pies. The plant was an important food and medicinal source for Native Americans, who also fashioned the stems into flutes and arrow shafts. Elderberries tend to form thickets that commonly reach heights of 12–15 feet. The flower and berry clusters sit conspicuously at the top of the foliage.

## River Cane (*Arundinaria gigantean*)

Arundinaria is the only genera of bamboo native to North America. Growing in expansive, dense stands known as canebrakes, it was once the dominant plant along Georgia's rivers, but today scientist believe that it occupies less than 5 percent of its original range due to agriculture, grazing, fire suppression, and urbanization. It propagates primarily through rhizomes, with these spreading roots leading to the impenetrable canebrakes. The demise of river cane has likely contributed to the pollution of our streams, as it plays a critical role in slowing stormwater and filtering pollutants. Native Americans used the plant for nearly everything, fashioning it into spears, arrows, baskets, homes, mats, knives, torches, rafts, tubes, and drills.

## River Oats
### (Chasmanthium latifolium)

This 2-to-4-foot-tall native grass is distinguished by its seed head clusters that resemble flattened oats. In the summer, these clusters are bright green, but with the fall they turn brownish tan along with the plant's grasslike leaves. Like other riparian vegetation, it plays a critical role in stabilizing stream banks and minimizing erosion. It also serves as food for many songbirds.

## Sensitive Fern (Onoclea sensibilis)

This shade-loving fern is found in floodplain forests along rivers and streams as well as in swamps and marshes. To the untrained eye, the fronds of this fern may look very unfernlike because of the generous space between lobes. By late summer, fertile fronds arise that resemble an elongated cluster of dark brown beads on a stalk. Like many ferns, the leaves of the sensitive fern contain toxins that dissuade grazing by deer.

## Cinnamon Fern (Osmunda cinnamomea)

Cinnamon fern flourishes where its roots remain wet; thus it is a common fern along the river's edge. A large fern, it sends up several fronds in a palmlike whorl that reach 5 feet in length. The fertile fronds (cinnamon-colored stalks bearing the plant's spores) rise from the center of the whorl. In early spring, the young, hairy fiddleheads are a culinary treat for both humans and beasts, and hummingbirds are known to line their nests with the "hair" that covers this early growth. Fossilized fern specimens resembling cinnamon ferns date back 220 million years.

## Privet (*Ligustrum sinense*)

Next to kudzu, perhaps no other invasive plant has done more to alter Georgia's woodlands. A native of China, privet was introduced into the United States in 1852 for use as an ornamental shrub. By the mid-20th century, it had escaped domestic cultivation and spread throughout Georgia. It can grow to 30 feet in height and, owing to its ability to spread via seeds and sprouts, it forms dense thickets, outcompeting native species like river cane. Once established, it is very difficult to remove.

Its berries are eaten by many songbirds (which unfortunately further disperse the seeds), and beavers like the bark. Privet sports sickly-sweet-smelling white blooms in the spring and summer, which produce blue-black berries that persist on the plant into the winter.

## Cardinal Flower (*Lobelia cardinalis*)

From July through September, it is difficult to find a Georgia river that does not have the tall slender green stalks of cardinal flower topped by a cluster of brilliant red blooms along its banks. The stalks can grow to up to 4 feet in height and are common along the base of the riverbank. A lover of moist soils, some have even been seen growing in cavities of partially submerged logs. Their common name is derived from the colored vestments worn by cardinals of the Roman Catholic Church. That color makes the plant irresistible to hummingbirds, which, along with bees and butterflies, are the flower's primary pollinators.

# Aquatic Plants

## Riverweed/Threadfoot (*Podostemum ceratophyllum*)

This inconspicuous and highly specialized aquatic plant grows on rocks and boulders on the river bottom in swift-moving shoals, rapids, and waterfalls of Georgia rivers above the fall line. Its threadlike masses have an unusual rubbery, seaweed-like texture sporting many narrow olive-green leaves. It plays an important role in stream ecology by providing habitat and food for aquatic insects that form the base of a river's food chain.

## Water Willow (*Justicia Americana*)

This perennial aquatic wildflower is common along river, stream, and lake margins and is often seen in large, dense colonies. Grasslike, its has leaves very similar to those of the black willow tree, but its white-to-pale-purple orchidlike blooms with purple streaks on the lower petals make this plant easy to identify. The blooms that appear throughout the summer are born at the top of long (up to 3 feet) slender stems. Another important plant for the river's macro invertebrate community, mammals also make use of it. Deer browse the leaves, while beaver and muskrat consume the plant's rhizomes.

## Pennsylvania Smartweed (*Polygonum pensylvanicum*)

There are more than a dozen native species of smartweed in Georgia, with Pennsylvania smartweed being one of the most important for waterfowl, songbirds, and mammals. Stands of smartweed provide cover for young waterfowl, and the shiny black seeds produced in the late summer provide food for those waterfowl and dozens of other birds. Muskrats, raccoons, and fox squirrels also feast on the seeds and the plants themselves. The white-to-light-pink blooms of smartweed are born on spikes at the end of stems.

# Species Endemic to the Etowah River

## Etowah Darter (*Etheostoma etowahae*)

Found in the Etowah River basin, and nowhere else in the world, this federally endangered fish inhabits small riffles and rapids where the streambed is filled with gravel and small pebbles. It has been identified in the mainstem of the Etowah and in Amicalola Creek, Shoal Creek in Dawson County, Long Swamp Creek, Yellow Creek, Smithwick Creek, Stamp Creek, and Raccoon Creek. It reaches lengths of up to 3 inches, and during the summer spawning it sports brilliant red and blue markings on its fins and tail.

## Cherokee Darter
## (*Etheostoma scotti*)

A federally threatened fish, Cherokee darters live in the small streams feeding the Etowah (and nowhere else in the world). They are small members of the perch family (not reaching more than 3 inches in length) and sport dark saddles on their backs and sides. During spawning season, males show red bands in the fins. They are commonly found in shallow pools and runs over gravel and large rocks.

## Holiday Darter
## (*Etheostoma brevirostrum*)

So named because of the brilliant, red, green, and blue markings that males show during the spawning season of the spring and early summer, holiday darters are found only in highest reaches of Amicalola Creek and the Etowah River. In fact, the population found in the Etowah is believed to be genetically different from those found in the Amicalola. They grow to lengths of about two and a half inches and are listed as "threatened" by Georgia's Department of Natural Resources.

## Etowah Crayfish (*Cambarus (Hiaticambarus) fasciatus*)

One of Georgia's 73 species of crayfish, the Etowah is believed to be restricted to the river basin above Lake Allatoona. It grows to a maximum length of 3 inches and is brown with red markings on the edges of the abdomen. Its tail may include a tinge of blue. Its preferred habitat is shelter beneath rocks and woody debris in swift-moving areas of streams.

# Protecting the Etowah

If you have put this book to use by exploring the Etowah, you can cite dozens of reasons to protect the river and its tributaries.

Unfortunately, just a small portion of
Georgia's population is as lucky as you,
but even those who have never set foot or
paddle in this river need do little more
than look around to find a million reasons
to protect it—the one million residents
who depend upon the Etowah for all, or a
portion, of their drinking water supply.

That, coupled with the fact that the
Etowah has more imperiled species than
any other river system of its size in the
southeastern United States, is ample
incentive to save the Etowah.

Dams, pollution, and water diversions
all threaten this biological and recreation-
al gem that is the lifeblood for communities that lie along its banks.

You can protect the Etowah by getting involved in one of the organizations listed
below. Make a contribution to support their efforts, volunteer as a water monitor, get
involved in a river cleanup, learn about Georgia's laws protecting our rivers, report
problems when you see them, engage elected officials in supporting laws that protect
our rivers, and tell your friends and neighbors about the treasure that is the Etowah.

Can one person make a difference? You bet, and the river teaches us how. The
spring that begins the Etowah, in and of itself, is but a trickle of water—enough to
fill the canteen of a backpacker, yet by the time the young Etowah has traveled less
than a mile, it is joined by dozens of other trickles. The combined force of these
waters has carved and etched a path out of the mountains. As other tributaries join
the flow, a mighty movement forms—an unstoppable force that feeds a million.

Likewise, the lives we lead and the choices we make can create a mighty movement—one that cherishes and protects the Etowah.

Coosa River Basin Initiative /
Upper Coosa Riverkeeper
408 Broad St.
Rome GA 30161
706-232-2724
www.coosa.org

Upper Etowah River Alliance
P.O. Box 307
Canton GA 30169
www.etowahriver.org

Georgia River Network
126 S. Milledge Ave.
Suite E3
Athens GA 30605
706-549-4508
www.garivers.org

Georgia Water Coalition
www.garivers.org/gawater

Mountain Conservation Trust
of Georgia
104 North Main St.
Suite B3
Jasper GA 30143
706-253-4077
www.mctga.org

The Georgia Conservancy
817 West Peachtree St.
Suite 200
Atlanta GA 30308
404-876-2900
www.georgiaconservancy.org

Georgia Sierra Club
743 E. College Ave, Suite B
Decatur GA 30030
404-607-1262
www.georgia.sierraclub.org

Georgia Wildlife Federation
11600 Hazelbrand Rd.
Covington GA 30014
770-787-7887
www.gwf.org

The Nature Conservancy
1330 West Peachtree St. NW
Suite 410
Atlanta GA 30309
404-873-6946
www.nature.org

# Photo Credits

All photos are by Joe Cook except the following, for which the author thanks the photographers:

Brett Albanese: 134 bottom

R. D. Bartlett: 136 bottom

Steven J. Baskauf, http://bioimages .vanderbilt.edu: 142 left and right; 143 left and right; 144 left and right; 145 right; 146 right; 147 left and right; 148 left and right; 149 bottom right; 151 top and bottom right

Giff Beaton: 131 bottom; 132 top and middle; 141 top and middle

Alan Cressler: 157 top

EIC, used under Creative Commons license 3.0: 128 middle

Kevin Enge: 137 bottom

Arlyn W. Evans: 157 bottom

Bud Freeman: 158 middle

Cris Hagen: 138

Ty Ivey: 132 bottom

John Jensen: 129 bottom

Steven G. Johnson, used under Creative Commons license 3.0: 135 middle

Phillip Jordan: 128 bottom; 129 top; 130 bottom; 133 middle and bottom; 134 top; 145 left

Thomas Luhring: 136 top

Chris Lukhaup: 159

Linda May, Georgia DNR: 149 top and bottom left

James H. Miller: 153 bottom

James H. Miller and Ted Bodner: 150 top, middle, and bottom; 152 bottom; 154; 156 top and bottom

Hugh and Carol Nourse: 152 top left, center, and right; 153 top; 155 top; 157 middle

Richard Orr: 140 middle; 141 bottom

Robert Potts, © California Academy of Sciences: 127 top

Todd Schneider, Georgia DNR, Wildlife Resources Division: 146 left; 151 bottom left; 155 middle and bottom

David E. Scott: 135 top and bottom

Terry Spivey, USDA Forest Service, Bugwood.org: 129 middle

David Stone: 140 bottom

Amos Tuck: 158 bottom

Robert Wayne Van Devender: 137 top and middle

Jess Van Dyke: 139 top

Daniel F. Vickers: 127 bottom; 128 top; 131 top left and top right; 133 top

Deb Weiler: 158 top

Whatcom County Noxious Weed Board: 139 bottom

Tom Wilson: 130 top and middle

Jason Wisniewski: 139 middle

Robert T. Zappalorti: 136 middle